Praise for *The Cognitive Beha*

'The first edition of this book was a quintessential introductory text on the history, science and practice of cognitive behavioural therapy. This second edition is even better – thoroughly updated, informed by the latest research and clinical applications and expertly illustrated with clinical examples. This is a trusted guide for therapists, counsellors, psychologists and health professionals in training.'
Dr Gillian Todd is a Fellow of the British Association of Behavioural & Cognitive Psychotherapies and a BABCP & EABCT accredited CBT practitioner, supervisor and trainer

Praise for the first edition

'This small book has it all. It explains CBT perfectly, and also helps practitioners in knowing what to expect and how to do therapy, manage patients' expectations and help their patients achieve their goals. It also helps a lot with written assignments for whoever is doing any CBT, counselling or other therapy courses.'
Online reviewer

'This is an excellent and clear overview of cognitive behavioural therapy. The process of therapy is clearly explained using examples to illustrate specific points. I also like the 'thumbnail' description of the philosophical and theoretical background to the approach. We recommend this book to all learners on our courses (therapists, counsellors, social workers, nurses etc.).'
Online reviewer

'Short but packed with practical, eye-opening ideas. All the basics of CBT in one small book.'
Online reviewer

'Brilliant book for doing a foundation degree in integrative counselling. Easy to read and understand, well set out and I have found it useful for assignments. Most of my class have now bought it.'
Online reviewer

The Cognitive Behaviour Therapy Primer

second edition

**Rhena Branch, Jodie Paget
and Windy Dryden**

First published in 2008
This edition published in 2021

PCCS Books Ltd
Wyastone Business Park
Wyastone Leys
Monmouth
NP25 3SR
UK

Tel +44 (0)1600 891509
contact@pccs-books.co.uk
www.pccs-books.co.uk

© Rhena Branch, Jodie Paget and Windy Dryden, 2021
Series introduction © Pete Sanders, 2021

All rights reserved.
No part of this publication may be reproduced, stored in a retrieval system, transmitted or utilised in any form by any means, electronic, mechanical, photocopying or recording or otherwise without permission in writing from the publishers.

The authors have asserted their right to be identified as the authors of this work in accordance with the Copyright, Designs and Patents Act 1988.

The Cognitive Behaviour Therapy Primer (second edition)

A CIP catalogue record for this book is available from the British Library.

ISBNs paperback 978 1 910919 98 9
       epub 978 1 910919 99 6

Cover design by Jason Anscomb
Printed in the UK by Severn, Gloucester

Contents

	Series introduction – *Pete Sanders*	*1*
1.	The origins of cognitive behaviour therapy	*7*
2.	The theoretical underpinnings of cognitive behaviour therapy	*16*
3.	Cognition	*27*
4.	Cognitive behaviour therapy and the therapeutic alliance	*36*
5.	Case conceptualisation	*44*
6.	Cognitive restructuring techniques	*52*
7.	Behavioural techniques	*65*
8.	Methods of discovering assumptions, rules and core beliefs	*78*
9.	Relapse prevention and endings	*92*
10.	Cognitive behaviour therapy transcript	*100*
11	Applications and developments in cognitive behaviour therapy	*112*
12	Research into cognitive behaviour therapy	*118*
	Appendix 1: Resources for learning	*125*
	Appendix 2: Relapse prevention worksheet	*127*
	Glossary	*131*
	References	*137*
	Index	*143*

Author biographies

Rhena Branch is a BABCP accredited practitioner, supervisor and trainer. She has lectured at Goldsmith's University of London, Anglia Ruskin University and the University of East Anglia. She has written several books on the subject of CBT and REBT. Rhena has a private practice in Norfolk and is director and clinical lead of a mental health charity serving Norfolk and Suffolk.

Jodie Paget is a BABCP accredited practitioner, trainer and supervisor. She has worked as a lecturer and supervisor at the University of East Anglia. She currently has a private practice in Norfolk and is co-director and clinical lead of a mental health charity in Norfolk.

Windy Dryden is Emeritus Professor of Psychotherapeutic Studies at Goldsmiths University, London, and is a Fellow of the British Psychological Society. He has authored or edited more than 250 books, including the second edition of *Reason to Change: A rational emotive behaviour therapy (REBT) workbook* (2021) and the third edition of *Rational Emotive Behaviour Therapy: Distinctive features* (forthcoming). In addition, he edits 21 book series in the area of counselling, psychotherapy and coaching, including the *CBT Distinctive Features* series. His major interests are in rational emotive behavior therapy and CBT; single-session interventions; the interface between counselling and coaching; pluralism in counselling and psychotherapy; writing short, accessible self-help books for the general public, and demonstrating therapy live in front of an audience.

Series introduction
Pete Sanders

Cognitive behaviour therapy (CBT) is one of many different types of 'talking therapy'. It is an active-directive, collaborative approach to dealing with emotional and psychiatric disorders. This means that CBT therapists talk directly to their clients and ask them direct questions. It also means that the client and therapist work together in a very overt manner to help the former overcome their presenting difficulties.

In contrast to psychodynamic, psychoanalytical or person-centred schools of therapy, CBT is focused on the present, meaning much of the therapeutic work undertaken is on specific beliefs and behaviours that are maintaining current problems, as opposed to discussion about the development of such beliefs, although this is also addressed when necessary. CBT is time bound, meaning the number of sessions is known to both patient and therapist. CBT is highly structured, with specific items addressed within a session that are known to be relevant to the main problem(s) that brought the person to therapy. CBT is goal orientated, meaning specific goals are identified early on and reviewed frequently.

This is not to imply that the other therapeutic modalities mentioned are not interested in structure and goals, but that CBT addresses these in a very obvious fashion. In CBT treatment, it is not uncommon for the therapist to do at least half of the talking. Long silences are not considered to be therapeutically valid in most cases and the client will often be interrupted and redirected by the therapist in the interest of retaining focus. Between-session homework assignments are also used extensively in order to maximise therapeutic gain. As the name suggests, CBT between-session work targets both cognitive and behavioural factors that perpetuate and maintain psychological disorders.

This book is specifically aimed at people wanting to learn about CBT who have little or no previous experience or knowledge of counselling or psychology. Despite its name, CBT belongs firmly within the counselling family and is practised by talking therapists of all schools: psychotherapists (or therapists), psychologists and counsellors. So, before we launch into a detailed discussion and explanation of cognitive behavioural ways of working, it might be helpful to take a look at counselling itself: what it is, what it is for, how it works and how it can be helpful.

What is counselling for?

One way of defining counselling is to look at what it is useful for. In the past 30 years, counselling has become ubiquitous, and it is perilously close to being presented as a panacea for just about everything. Some critics say that the emerging 'profession' of counselling has much to gain from claiming, on behalf of counsellors and therapists, that counselling is good for everything. It would be wrong to make such claims: counselling has its limits and part of being a counsellor is to know what those limits are. The problem is that when we are in distress, it is comforting to think that there is a simple answer around the corner.

The situation is not made any easier when we understand that simply sitting down and taking time out from a busy life can make things seem better. Counsellors must be able to explain to their clients the differences between this very important relief and comfort that can be gained from compassionate human contact on the one hand, and counselling as a specialist activity on the other. Counselling can help people in certain states of distress and usually involves change:

- change in the way a client sees things or themselves
- change in the way a client thinks about things or themselves
- change in the way a client feels about things or themselves
- change in the way a client behaves.

Although many people will not be able to put it neatly into a few words, what they seek from counselling can be roughly summarised in a few categories:

- support
- recovery
- problem-solving
- gaining insight or self-awareness
- developing new strategies for living.

The sort of distress that counselling can help is often called 'emotional' or 'psychological' and can include:

- stress – a very general and possibly over-used term, but there are some situations in life, especially those that you can't control, that might leave you feeling so stressed that it interferes with your everyday life
- conflict – at home or work
- bereavement – whether a relative or friend. Indeed, having anything permanently taken away might lead to a feeling of bereavement, such as losing your job or losing your ability to do something like walk, play sport or have sex
- depression – another over-used term and not one to be taken lightly. Many life events can make us feel low, and talking it over really does help. The popular term 'depression' can cover everything from feeling understandably low after having your purse stolen or losing your job, through to being unable to get up in the morning or eat properly because you think life is not worth living
- coping with poor health – e.g. having a long-standing

health problem or receiving a diagnosis of a serious or terminal illness
- trauma – e.g. surviving (including witnessing) something very disturbing (including abuse of various forms).

What counselling is not for

When someone decides to attend counselling sessions, they are, by definition, distressed. It is, therefore, particularly important that the client doesn't have either their time wasted or their distress increased by attending something that we might reasonably predict would be of no help.

As we have already seen, it is difficult to honestly predict whether counselling will definitely help in a particular circumstance. Nevertheless there are times when counselling is clearly not the first or only appropriate intervention. It is doubly difficult to appear to turn someone away when they arrive because sometimes:

- part of their distress might be that they have difficulty feeling understood and valued
- they may lack self-confidence and a rejection would damage it even more
- they have been to other types of helper and they think that counselling is their last hope
- they are so desperate they might consider suicide.

However difficult it might be, we have to be completely honest with clients if we think counselling is not going to help. It would be wrong to let them find out after a number of sessions, after which they might feel that they are to blame for not trying hard enough. The use of counselling should be questioned if it is likely that their symptoms of distress are caused by external factors, such as poor housing or homelessness; lack of opportunity due to discrimination or oppression, or poverty.

Problems of this nature are best addressed by social action. The counsellor as a citizen shares responsibility with all other members of society to remove these blocks to people's physical and psychological wellbeing.

It would be convenient if we could divide problems up into two neat categories: those of psychological origin (and amenable to counselling) and those of non-psychological origin (and therefore not amenable to counselling). However, there are some other causes of distress that, although they will not be solved by counselling, will undoubtedly be helped by counselling in that the person concerned will be able to function better with the kind of support that counselling can provide. It may also be that the client experiences repetitive patterns of self-defeating thoughts and behaviour that renders them less effective in dealing with problems that do not have a psychological origin. It might also be that a person would be better able to challenge an oppressive system if they felt personally empowered, and counselling can sometimes achieve this. Such problems include those caused by:

- poor health (a physical illness or organic condition)
- oppression and discrimination, including bullying
- living in an abusive relationship.

Counsellors must be constantly vigilant to ensure that their work with a particular client or clients in general is not contributing to disadvantage, abuse and oppression by rendering people more acceptant of poor conditions, whether at work or at home.

Psychologists must join with persons who reject racism, sexism, colonialism and exploitation and must find ways to redistribute social power and to increase social justice. Primary prevention research inevitably will make clear the relationship between social pathology and psycopathology and then will work to change social and political structures in the interests of social justice. It is as simple and as difficult as that! (Albee, 1996, p.1131, cited in Davies & Burdett, 2004, p.279)

What is 'personal growth'?

Counselling in the UK has become associated with what might

be called the 'personal growth industry'. Self-improvement has been a feature of our society for a hundred years or more and includes such initiatives as the Workers' Education Association supporting the educational needs of working men and women. More recently, further education has embraced more non-vocational courses and reflects the fact that, as we get more affluent, we have to attend less to the business of mere survival. We can turn our attention to getting more out of life, and, along with other self-development activities, improving our psychological wellbeing proves to be a popular choice. Furthermore, when people have a good experience as a client, they sometimes see that learning to be a counsellor could be a further step in self-improvement.

This 'personal growth' use of counselling contrasts with counselling as a treatment for more acute forms of psychological distress, as described above. It is, however, no less worthy or useful. Fulfilled, happy citizens, relating positively to themselves and others and able to put good helping skills back into their communities, are an asset, not a handicap.

Using the glossary

Throughout this book, you will find some words are set in SMALL CAPITALS. This indicates that the glossary at the end of the book carries a brief definition and explanation of the term.

Client work

Unless otherwise indicated, details of clients have been changed and disguised throughout this book to ensure anonymity.

Chapter 1
The origins of cognitive behaviour therapy

COGNITIVE behaviour therapy (CBT) has arisen from diverse theoretical foundations. In this chapter we will discuss some of the most relevant historical influences that have informed and shaped its development.

Historical context

The field of psychology was dominated in the mid-20th century by BEHAVIOURISM and PSYCHOANALYSIS. These two monolithic schools had little in common. Behaviourists attached little importance to the internal workings of an individual's mind and considered that the external environment determined behaviour. Psychoanalysts, on the other hand, considered the internal world of paramount importance – but also largely unconscious and therefore hidden from the individual. Therefore, a trained analyst was needed to guide the client towards insight. Neither of these schools placed particular emphasis on commonplace, readily accessible thoughts such as those that feature prominently in present-day CBT.

However, from BEHAVIOURISM and PSYCHOANALYSIS emerged several professionals with a burgeoning interest in the mediating role of COGNITION between stimulus and response.

In the 1950s, Albert Ellis became dissatisfied with the results he was getting using PSYCHOANALYSIS with his patients. He turned his attention to developing his own therapeutic approach, based on his clinical experience and extensive knowledge of human psychology. Thus, rational emotive therapy (RET) was born (Ellis, 1994). Ellis's views on treating human disturbance were quite radical at the time. PSYCHOANALYSIS dominated and recognition of RET was hard won. Ellis successfully used RET to treat clients with emotional disorders and sexual problems. In later years, the name was changed to rational emotive behaviour therapy (REBT) to accurately reflect the behavioural component of this approach.

Aaron T. Beck, who also came from a PSYCHOANALYTICAL background, responded to Ellis's innovations in psychotherapy and, in the 1970s, founded COGNITIVE therapy (CT) (Beck, 1976). Through the continued work of Beck, Ellis and others, CT evolved and developed to become COGNITIVE behaviour therapy (CBT), as we know it today.

Donald Meichenbaum also developed his own approach, called self-instructional training (SIT) (Meichenbaum, 1985). Meichenbaum started out as a behaviourist. All three approaches drew on information gained from the behaviourist movement and early behavioural experiments, while giving COGNITION a central role. COGNITIVE psychology became more widely accepted due to validating research outcomes and changes within the behaviourist camp. By the 1970s, COGNITIVE psychology was beginning to truly flourish.

Behaviour therapy influences on CBT

The historical influences of present-day CBT stretch back to the beginning of the 20th century and Pavlov's work on CLASSICAL CONDITIONING (1927), which provided roots for the development of behaviour therapy. Although Pavlov's experiments involved animal subjects, the assumption was that the principles derived from work with animals could be reasonably applied to humans. CLASSICAL CONDITIONING arose from Pavlov's well-known experiment with dogs.

Food is an *unconditioned stimulus* and salivation is an *unconditioned response*; dogs produce saliva at the sight of food without being taught to do so. Pavlov experimented by sounding a bell immediately before presenting the dogs with food. The introduction of the bell had an interesting effect on the unconditioned response of salivation. After several repetitions of combining food with the sound of the bell, the dogs began to salivate just on hearing the bell. Hence, the sound of the bell (*conditioned stimulus*) elicited salivation (*conditioned response*). Pavlov also investigated the effects of removing the unconditioned stimulus (food) when the bell was sounded. He found that, over time, the conditioned response (salivation) ceased.

Around the same time, Thorndike (1898) and others were developing OPERANT CONDITIONING. Thorndike experimented using cats. The cats were placed in a box where the only means of escape came from pulling a loop. Once the cats came to associate the pulling of the loop with escape, they were able to escape more quickly. OPERANT CONDITIONING holds that behaviour is largely determined by consequences. Hence the desirable result of escape reinforces the loop-pulling behaviour. As Pavlov discovered with his dogs and the erosion of their response to the bell, once the reinforcing consequence (escape) was removed, eventually the cats' associated behaviour (loop-pulling) also ceased.

These new learning models were later applied to experiments using human subjects. MALADAPTIVE BEHAVIOURS were created and subsequently eliminated using the learning principles of both CLASSICAL and OPERANT CONDITIONING. Controversially, infants and children were frequently the subjects of these experiments. Although seminal experiments such as that of Watson and Rayner (1920) would not make it past an ethics board today, their work provided much insight into the mechanics of human behaviour. Watson and Rayner worked with a nine-month-old baby boy, known as 'Little Albert'. Little Albert was repeatedly shown a white rat while simultaneously being subjected to a loud, disturbing noise. After several repetitions of the appearance of a white rat accompanied by the distressing sound, Little Albert responded with fear at the sight of the rat alone. His fear response then quickly generalised to almost any white object resembling a rat, such as a swatch of white fur. From this experiment, Watson and Rayner concluded that irrational fears or phobias were conditioned emotional responses to specific stimuli.

In the 1950s, Burrhus Fredric Skinner and Joseph Wolpe were working independently on further advancing the learning theories borne out of Pavlov's and Thorndike's earlier contributions. Skinner invented an OPERANT CONDITIONING chamber, commonly referred to as 'Skinner's box', when he was a Harvard graduate student in the 1930s. Skinner used animal subjects in the main and looked closely at rule-governed behaviour. He focused on the effects of positive reinforcement more than on punishment/negative reinforcement. Skinner found that behaviours reinforced by a positive outcome (such as the delivery of food) were readily and consistently adopted by his animal subjects.

Joseph Wolpe introduced systematic desensitisation in 1958. He worked on the assumption that, if ANXIETY responses could be legitimately considered conditioned responses (as asserted by Watson and Rayner), then a subject could theoretically be de-conditioned. Through habitual exposure to a conditioned stimulus without a negative reinforcer, the conditioned fear response should eventually erode. Around the time of Wolpe, and in part due to his influence, behaviour therapy increasingly incorporated COGNITIVE VARIABLES into its approach.

In the late 1960s and early 1970s, Albert Bandura (Bandura, 1977a, 1977b) laid down important stepping stones towards an increased emphasis on COGNITIVE processes in behavioural therapy and clinical intervention. Bandura's social learning theory and behavioural modification approaches emphasised COGNITION as integral to behaviour acquisition and adjustment. In essence, he disputed the traditional 'stimulus leads to response' paradigm, and instead asserted that the individual has reciprocal influence on the environmental stimulus. Bandura was among the first to recognise COGNITIVE factors as pivotal to understanding learned behaviour. Social learning theory gave rise to COGNITIVE reconceptualisation among several of

Bandura's learning-theorist contemporaries. This revolution in thinking provided a springboard for the manifestation of COGNITIVE theory and associated therapeutic orientations.

That said, however, Albert Ellis (who was previously a psychoanalyst) had in fact been convinced that COGNITIVE VARIABLES mediated behaviour (based on his clinical experience) from as early as 1957. Aaron Beck began his own investigation into COGNITIVE aspects of depression in the early 1960s, drawing somewhat on Ellis's theories. Yet it wasn't until the early 1970s that COGNITIVE therapeutic approaches gained true recognition. At this stage, behavioural and COGNITIVE theory seem to have merged sufficiently to radicalise psychotherapeutic practice.

In addition to those mentioned in this section, several other psychologists made significant contributions toward the advancement and development of COGNITIVE models. There is an excellent review of the historical basis of COGNITIVE behavioural treatments in Dobson and Block (1988), and two comprehensive chapters on the subject in Clark et al. (1999).

Philosophical underpinnings of CBT

Greek stoic philosophers devoted much thought to the SUBJECTIVE EXPERIENCE of reality. Much of stoical teaching emphasises the role of idiosyncratic meaning in defining human experience. Early philosophers such as Epictetus, Cicero, Seneca and Aurelius are well known for positing the notion that COGNITIVE VARIABLES mediate and determine emotional responses to events. Although they did not state these philosophies in such overtly scientific terms, the basic sentiment is represented in various sayings attributed to them, such as 'Man is not affected by events but by the view he takes of them' (Epictetus). The philosophical foundations of present-day CBT are also interlaced in the works of later philosophers such as Heidegger and Hegel.

Cognitive therapy influences on CBT

The term 'COGNITIVE therapy' currently refers to a multitude of models accounting for human distress and a spectrum of associated interventions (see Figure 1.1). It is a common misconception that CBT theory proposes that thoughts cause feelings and behaviours; in fact, it considers them to reciprocally influence each other. In other words, CBT places emphasis on the interaction and multidirectional relationship between COGNITIVE, behavioural and physiological realms. COGNITION and behaviour reciprocally influence one another to shape an individual's understanding and experience of his or her environment. Equally, emotions, environment and physiology influence COGNITION and behaviour.

The CBT viewpoint of a highly reciprocal interactive system informs choice of intervention when dealing with psychological disturbance. Interventions are typically aimed at both dysfunctional COGNITION and dysfunctional behaviour. Thus CBT could simply be considered a hybrid between COGNITIVE and behavioural therapies. More accurately, however, CBT has developed from a more complex amalgam of behaviour therapy and three distinct seminal schools of COGNITIVE therapy (Rachman & Wilson, 1980), as already mentioned above. We now briefly describe these schools.

Rational emotive behaviour therapy

The first school is Ellis's rational emotive therapy (RET), or rational emotive behaviour therapy (REBT) as it is now known. REBT posits that IRRATIONAL BELIEFS are at the core of emotional disturbance and that RATIONAL BELIEFS lead to functional emotional responses to adverse experiences. Characteristics of both types of beliefs are outlined below.

REBT uses an ABC MODEL wherein A denotes an ACTIVATING EVENT that is mediated by beliefs (B), which significantly influence specific emotional, behavioural and COGNITIVE consequences (C). Treatment involves helping the client to identify their IRRATIONAL BELIEFS, and challenge and modify them. Belief modification is achieved through various interventions, including direct DISPUTATION of irrational thinking, behavioural testing of the validity and utility of beliefs, COGNITIVE RESTRUCTURING exercises and various homework tasks.

Irrational beliefs	Rational beliefs
Rigid and extreme	Flexible and non-extreme
Inconsistent with reality	Consistent with reality
Illogical	Logical
Unhelpful/impeding	Pragmatic/promote problem-solving

Cognitive therapy

The second of these influential schools of therapy is Beck's COGNITIVE therapy (CT). Although Beck developed CT independently of RET/REBT, they share similar presumptions about the development and maintenance of psychological disturbance. REBT focuses primarily on the effect of IRRATIONAL BELIEFS on the appraisal of events and consequent emotions and behaviours. Faulty interpretations are considered a by-product of IRRATIONAL BELIEFS and therefore are typically reassessed only after belief change has taken place. CT typically homes in on the distorted content of the appraisal itself. Distorted interpretations, usually referred to as NEGATIVE AUTOMATIC THOUGHTS (NATS) in CBT (or inferences in REBT), are challenged and modified using techniques similar to those used in REBT. Homework tasks are also a central feature of CT, with the emphasis on achieving INFERENTIAL change. For a more detailed discussion on the differences between CBT and REBT, see Padesky & Beck (2003, 2005) and Ellis (2005).

Self-instructional training

Meichenbaum's self-instructional training (SIT) is the third school of influence. Meichenbaum derived his model of therapy from Ellis's RET and from his own work using operant instruction with people diagnosed with schizophrenia (Meichenbaum, 1969). Those who were able to give themselves covert self-instruction were found to perform better at tasks than those who did not self-instruct. SIT is essentially a skills-acquisition model that incorporates techniques such as modification of negative self-talk and development of coping strategies and problem-solving skills. There are six stages of SIT treatment (see also Meichenbaum, 1985):

1. defining problems
2. addressing identified problem areas
3. attention-focusing training
4. development of coping statements
5. COGNITIVE and behavioural error correction
6. self-reinforcement.

There are many theoretical and technical consistencies between these three psychotherapeutic approaches, despite variations in application. Although developed independently, all three have also influenced one another to some degree. Both REBT and CT in particular continue to wield considerable influence in the field of psychology. Beck's CT and therapy of depression (which he began developing in the 1960s) is particularly well researched and is responsible for ground-breaking impact on COGNITIVE psychology and psychology in general.

Conclusion

Many and varied approaches to dealing with psychological disorders are currently practised and fall under the broad heading of CBT. Despite some fundamental variations in theory and practice, all COGNITIVE approaches share some basic assumptions:

1. COGNITIONS exist.
2. COGNITIONS mediate psychological and behavioural problems.
3. Mediating COGNITIVE factors can be examined and changed.
4. Behavioural, emotional and COGNITIVE problems can be addressed via direct modification of dysfunctional mediating COGNITIONS.

For further information, you are recommended to follow up the sources cited in this chapter and listed in the references at the end of the book.

Figure 1.1: Historical antecedents of CBT

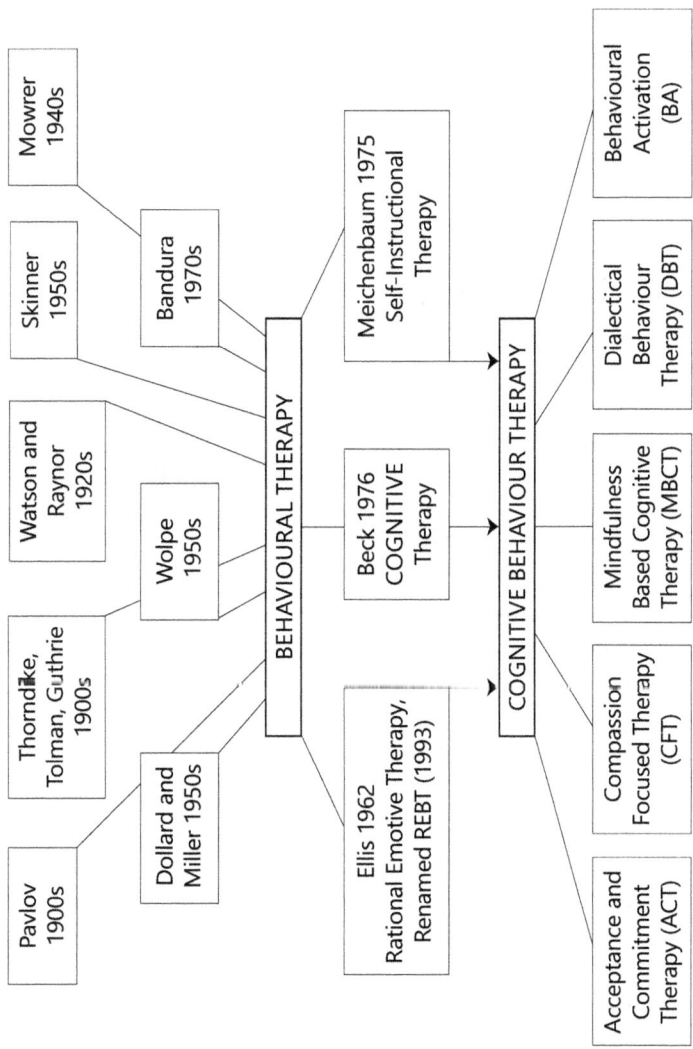

Chapter 2
The theoretical underpinnings of cognitive behaviour therapy

Thoughts and feelings

The main reason people pursue counselling is because they are experiencing emotional problems such as depression, ANXIETY, anger or guilt. Clients rarely arrive at the first session complaining about the way they think. They will typically describe their problems in one or more of the following ways:

- uncomfortable feelings that are impairing the client's daily functioning and/or enjoyment of life
- unsatisfactory life conditions, such as work stress, sleep disturbance, relationship difficulties, financial worries and so on
- negative life events, such as job loss, illness, relationship breakdown and traumatic incidents
- problematic behaviours, such as addiction, procrastination, AVOIDANCE, social withdrawal, loss of temper and so forth.

However, according to CBT theory, dysfunctional thinking is at the very heart of emotional disturbance. It is a commonly held assumption that other people's behaviour and undesirable external events directly cause us to feel negative emotions. While it is true that people generally feel badly when bad things happen,

CBT posits that these external conditions contribute to our negative emotions but are not solely or wholly responsible for causing emotional distress. Rather, according to CBT, how we interpret our experiences and appraise life events affects our emotional responses more profoundly than the event itself. The first-century CE philosopher Epictetus summed up this connection between thought and emotion with his now famous adage, 'Men are not disturbed by things but by the views which they take of them.'

Considering that any given individual's interpretations of what he or she experiences are by definition SUBJECTIVE, these are hypotheses or 'guesses' about reality, rather than solid 'facts' or evidence-based conclusions. Therefore, they may be OBJECTIVELY correct or incorrect to varying degrees. Hence, if an individual has persistent negative beliefs about himself and is given to particular styles of thinking errors (see Chapter 3), undue emotional disturbance is likely to follow negative events. Over time, such thinking will probably lead to emotional disorders, such as depression.

For example, a person may have a THINKING BIAS (or hold a false belief) that they are unlovable and worthless in an unfair and uncaring world. If they truly believe such negative appraisals of themselves and the world, it is easy to see how they may become depressed in the face of negative events, which they will construe as supporting evidence of their pre-existent belief system. To illustrate, imagine that three men (alike in most fundamental respects) are all unexpectedly rejected by a romantic partner. The first man feels very depressed about the rejection; the second feels ashamed, and the third is sad. How do we account for the fact that, in the face of the same event, these three individuals manifest entirely different emotions?

It all begins to make sense when we consider that, for the first man, the rejection proves 'I'm unlovable'; the second thinks, 'Who was I to think someone would want to love me? What a I fool I have been,' and the third says to himself, 'I really wanted things to work out with that person and it's a real shame it didn't, but I'll be okay.' Thus, three different ways of thinking about the rejection essentially produce three different ways of feeling.

The ABC model of CBT

Albert Ellis, who founded REBT, put two distinct types of beliefs – rational and irrational – at point B in the ABC MODEL (see Figure 2.1). According to Ellis, RATIONAL BELIEFS are flexible and non-extreme in nature, whereas IRRATIONAL BELIEFS are extreme and rigid in nature. RATIONAL BELIEFS tend to produce healthy, appropriate negative feelings in response to negative events and to promote problem-solving, self/other acceptance and healthy adjustment to undesired events or situations. Conversely, IRRATIONAL BELIEFS lead to unhealthy negative emotions, putting oneself or others down, impaired problem-solving and diminished adjustment in response to aversive events (Ellis, 1994). This concept is often referred to in CBT/REBT literature as the THOUGHT-FEELING LINK or the 'B–C connection'.

Returning to the example of the first man who felt depressed after being rejected by a romantic partner, we can conceptualise his depression using the ABC FORMAT as follows:

- Rejection by romantic partner (ACTIVATING EVENT).
- I absolutely should be loved by my romantic partner (irrational demand).
- It's awful that I am not loved by them (evaluation of 'awfulness').
- Not being loved by them proves that I'm totally unlovable (self-denigration).
- Depression (emotional consequence).
- Withdraws from usual activities that give pleasure (behavioural consequence).
- Ruminates on the factors he assumes or knows for sure contributed to the rejection and focuses on imagined future rejections (COGNITIVE consequences).

The theoretical underpinnings of cognitive behaviour therapy 19

We can also do an ABC on the second man's shame:

- Rejection by romantic partner (ACTIVATING EVENT).
- I should never have assumed I was attractive or lovable enough to sustain a relationship (irrational demand).
- It's terrible to have assumed this would have worked out/ that I was good enough (evaluation of 'awfulness').
- The ending of the relationship shows how much of a fool I am (self-denigration).
- Shame (emotional consequence).
- Avoids seeking or responding to support from friends and family (behavioural consequence).
- Imagines friends and family all agree he was punching above his weight (COGNITIVE consequences).

Using the ABC FORMAT again, we can see that the third man, who felt sad, held a rational preference that the relationship should continue and thus experienced a functional emotional response when it didn't work out:

- Rejection by romantic partner (ACTIVATING EVENT).
- I really wanted this relationship to work out but there's no reason that it absolutely had to do so (rational preference).
- It's sad that the relationship didn't work out but it's not the worst thing in the world (evaluation of 'badness').
- Being rejected by the person I desire just means, sadly, that they do not love me, but I am still a lovable person (self-acceptance).
- Sadness (emotional consequence).
- Continues to do activities that are enjoyable, engages in usual self-care activities (behavioural consequences).
- Doesn't dwell on recent break-up and is able to imagine finding love again in the future (COGNITIVE consequences).

Figure 2.1: The ABC model

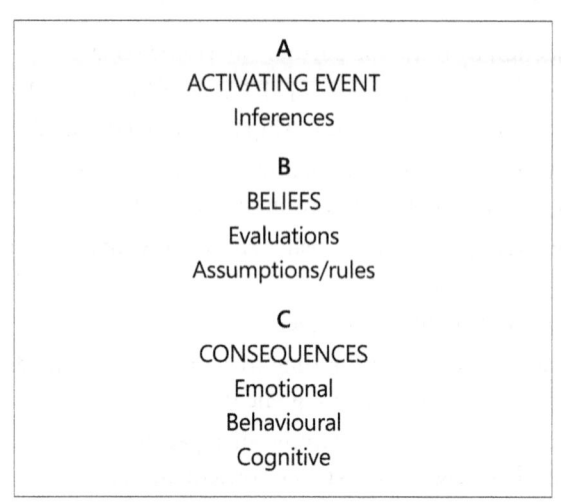

```
              A
      ACTIVATING EVENT
         Inferences

              B
           BELIEFS
          Evaluations
       Assumptions/rules

              C
        CONSEQUENCES
           Emotional
          Behavioural
           Cognitive
```

Functional and dysfunctional negative emotions

As already discussed in this chapter, CBT holds at its core the idea that our idiosyncratic interpretations and evaluations of our life experiences determine the quality of our negative emotional responses – healthy or unhealthy, ADAPTIVE or MALADAPTIVE. REBT holds with a QUALITATIVE (two continua) (Figure 2.2) versus QUANTITATIVE (single continuum) view of emotions (Figure 2.3). Unhealthy negative emotions are paired with a healthy alternative: for example, ANXIETY and concern. In REBT terms, ANXIETY stems from an IRRATIONAL BELIEF and is therefore unhealthy, whereas concern stems from a RATIONAL BELIEF and is considered healthy.

Figure 2.2: REBT separate continua

Concern

1 2 3 4 5 6 7 8 9 10

Anxiety

1 2 3 4 5 6 7 8 9 10

Figure 2.3: CBT single continuum

Concern							*Anxiety*		
1	2	3	4	5	6	7	8	9	10

While both types of negative emotion can be experienced with varying degrees of intensity (as represented by the LIKERT SCALE), healthy emotions such as concern are associated with ADAPTIVE BEHAVIOURAL and COGNITIVE consequences, but the unhealthy alternative (ANXIETY) will lead to MALADAPTIVE, problematic consequences.

However, most CBT therapists consider emotions to exist on a single continuum (Figure 2.3) and milder emotions are generally accepted as healthier, more functional alternatives to more extreme or intense feelings.

Perhaps the most significant benefit of Ellis's QUALITATIVE distinction between negative emotions is that it offers both therapists and clients a convenient, readily understandable construct for discerning between functional emotional distress and inappropriate or dysfunctional emotional disturbance/disorders. (A fuller explanation of the REBT perspective on human emotion can be found in Dryden (2021) and Dryden & Branch (2008.)

Characteristics of cognitive behaviour therapy

COGNITIVE therapy is usually thought of as a short-term therapy. It is true that CBT treatment is highly structured and incisive, thus lending itself nicely to short-term intervention. Many clients will improve in as few as 13 sessions, although this is dependent on several factors, such as the level of therapist competence, the severity and duration of the client's problem, environmental factors (unsatisfactory living circumstances, dysfunctional relationships, financial difficulties and so forth can impede therapeutic progress) and regular use of practical between-session assignments. Severe and chronic complaints may require long-term treatment and it is not unheard of for CBT treatment to span months or, more rarely, years. This is particularly likely when dealing with chronic depression, OBSESSIVE-COMPULSIVE DISORDER, personality disorders and other such manifestations of deep-rooted psychological disturbance.

Whatever the duration of treatment, the characteristics of CBT remain the same. Below is a breakdown of defining key features of CBT.

Time-limited

As already alluded to above, time-limited does not necessarily equate to 'brief'. However, the therapist will discuss treatment duration with the client in the initial sessions and, following a full assessment, will give an informed estimation of how many sessions are likely to be required. Regular reviews are used to determine the rate of progress. Most CBT therapists will suggest an initial review after about six sessions.

Structured

There are clear beginning, middle and end stages of CBT treatment. In the early stage, the client is introduced to the ABC MODEL, problems and goals are established and a conceptualisation formed. The bulk of the work takes place in the middle stage, when the problem list is worked through. Towards the end of treatment, the client is encouraged to take more control of sessions in preparation for acting as their own therapist post-discharge. They are also urged to consolidate useful learning through review and consistent practice. Relapse prevention is also discussed.

Agenda-based

Each session follows an agenda devised by client and therapist together. This helps maintain focus in the session and ensure best use is made of the time.

Active-directive

The therapist is active and directive throughout treatment. Questions are asked, DIDACTIC TEACHING takes place, points are debated and suggestions are offered. In-session discussion is typically shared between client and therapist. This differs from non-directive forms of therapy, where the client does the bulk of the talking.

Homework-based

Between-session tasks are a major part of CBT treatment. Because most clients have one hour-long session of therapy per week, it is important that they take new beliefs and behaviours acquired during sessions out into the real world. This progresses the therapeutic work from the intellectual to the experiential. The use of homework may well be the key factor that gives CBT its reputation for being efficient and long lasting.

Scientific

An experimental approach is taken to deal with client problems. Thoughts, attitudes, emotions and associated behaviours are delineated through the use of questionnaires and forms. Data are collected and examined, hypotheses are formulated, practical experiments devised and results evaluated. Additionally, CBT is well researched. Responsible therapists keep abreast of new findings, incorporating them into their existing practice as appropriate.

Collaborative

Client and therapist work side by side in an effort to resolve the client's difficulties. This promotes client independence and self-efficacy. Responsibility (and credit) for therapeutic gains is shared, although ultimately progress is attributed to the client's hard work.

Explicit

CBT is a 'cards-on-the-table' approach to dealing with psychological disturbance. Both client and therapist are equally aware of what is going on in sessions. Rather than keeping their interpretations of client belief systems to themselves, CBT therapists involve clients in open examination.

Psycho-educational

CBT therapists devote time to teaching the fundamentals of CBT and invite the client to share any questions, doubts and reservations they may have about core theory. DIDACTIC

TEACHING is part of the educative process but SOCRATIC QUESTIONING is also liberally used. SOCRATIC QUESTIONING is also known as 'guided discovery' (Beck et al., 1979; Padesky, 1993; Persons, 1989). Rather than telling the client what to think, questions are asked that lead the client to discover answers for themselves. It is posited that self-generated solutions are more deeply experienced and enduring.

Problem-focused

In the early sessions (if not in the initial session), clients are helped to devise a problem list. This may include emotional, behavioural and environmental difficulties that the client wants help to resolve. The therapist helps to refine the problem list by placing problems in categories and then asks the client to rank them in order of importance. Generally, problems that are most distressing or most interfere with day-to-day functioning are prioritised.

Goal-focused

For each item on the problem list, a goal is established. The goal will ideally include an emotional and a practical component. It is the therapist's job to ensure that goals are realistic and achievable. Goals will be reviewed regularly throughout treatment.

Ahistorical

CBT does not ignore the past, as has sometimes been said. Past experiences and childhood events are explored in CBT but with the precise aim of understanding how they may be reinforcing current problems. Client history is thus used to understand present difficulties and inform conceptualisation. Most of the therapeutic work is set in the present time. Unravelling and rehashing the past is not considered of fundamental therapeutic benefit and solutions are not considered to be hidden therein.

What a session of CBT looks like

Not every session of CBT looks exactly the same. However, the session structure is taught to trainees and most seasoned therapists will use an adaptation of it. Structure is invaluable for making the best use of the hour. It also helps the client to know what to expect from each session and therefore encourages them to arrive prepared. Bear in mind that, although they work in a way that is structured and focused, CBT therapists are not inflexible. In certain instances, for example, the agenda may be suspended in favour of dealing with a recent client crisis. If a client is highly agitated, distressed or suicidal, then these states will take precedence and will be addressed before returning to the typical agenda.

The following is a general guide to session format:

- greeting and mood check
- setting the agenda
- review of homework and previous session
- working through session objectives
- setting homework
- feedback on session.

First, the client is greeted and asked about their current mood. Information gathered here may prompt agenda items. Then agenda items are noted. This may involve the therapist or client writing on a white board. Items may include recent events, between-session practice, comments on the previous session, troubleshooting for future tasks or events, and emotional states. Homework review and feedback tend to be constant agenda items.

Learning outcomes from the previous session's homework are assessed. Obstacles to homework completion are investigated. If necessary, previously assigned homework is modified.

Problems the client would like to address in session are defined and worked through. ABC forms may well be used to identify faulty thinking and/or behaviour. Additional techniques such as imagery, role-play and DISPUTATION are also frequently used. Clients are encouraged to transfer learning from previously resolved problems to their current difficulties.

Based on session content, new homework is devised. Both client and therapist work to devise homework that is well suited to the client's problems. Opportunities to practise in-session learning and execute between-session tasks are identified. Often specific times for doing homework are scheduled into the client's week. This helps to ensure that tasks are carried out and not left to the last minute.

The client is invited to give feedback on their experience of the session and to ask questions. Any important issues raised will be added to the following session's agenda if time does not allow for immediate discussion.

CBT supervision

A further point of difference between CBT and other psychotherapies is the use of supervision by the therapist. Supervision is an opportunity for practitioners to present cases to an experienced therapist for advice and guidance on any topics relevant to the therapeutic work. While all psychotherapy practitioners are required to undertake supervision, the content of CBT supervision is not so much about the therapist's own personal development as it is in other psychotherapeutic modalities. Personal development is strongly encouraged in CBT via self-reflective practice and therapists can undergo their own therapy if they wish, but it is not as strongly encouraged, as it is in other modalities.

Furthermore, CBT therapists, especially in their training phases, will usually record sessions (using audio or video), and then play them back to the supervisor, rather than discuss with them what happened in the session. This allows supervisors to hear exactly what was said, how the client reacted, and what skills the supervisee is attempting to demonstrate. Assessment can be made by the supervisor regarding how closely the supervisee is adhering to the CBT model, which is essential if CBT is to continue being evidence-based. Detailed feedback can be given on what skills need to be refined and supervisors can demonstrate (through role play) how to practise specific skills (such as DISPUTING a negative belief).

In the following chapters we will look more closely at CBT theory and interventions.

Chapter 3
Cognition

Cognition

COGNITION is the 'C' in CBT. The *Oxford English Dictionary* defines COGNITION as:

- 'the mental action or process of acquiring knowledge and understanding through thought, experience, and the senses
- 'a perception, sensation, idea, or intuition resulting from the process of cognition.'

In CBT, the emphasis is on enhancing or developing ADAPTIVE COGNITION that helps the client adjust to altered circumstances, overcome aversive experiences and act in a constructive, goal-oriented manner. People with healthy beliefs (COGNITIONS) tend to experience fewer episodes of psychological disturbance and are therefore less likely to seek out therapy. Because of this point, much of CBT treatment focuses on eliciting and restructuring MALADAPTIVE goal-impeding thinking. In this chapter, we will explain the different categories of COGNITION that CBT recognises. People are highly idiosyncratic in the beliefs they hold and how they interpret the world around them. However, CBT research has investigated the ways people think to such an extent that recurrent themes have been identified. Below is a list of 12 THINKING BIASES (Burns, 1990) frequently demonstrated by people suffering from emotional problems such as depression and ANXIETY.

Cognitive distortions

1. All-or-nothing thinking

This describes how people can thinking in extremes, which often leads to extreme emotional and behavioural responses. For example, a situation is regarded as either wholly bad or wholly good, with no middle ground in between. Human experiences are rarely so stark.

2. Over-generalisation

Also referred to as the 'part-whole error', this involves forming global evaluations on the basis of one or more aspects of oneself or a situation. For example, you conclude you are a complete failure in your work having sent an email to your boss without the attachments you refer to in the email.

3. Mental filtering

This refers to an information-processing bias in which you only acknowledge information that fits with a pre-existing belief. For example, you believe you are unlovable and so overlook evidence to the contrary. The strongly held negative self-belief acts as a filter for one's experiences.

4. Mind-reading

This is the tendency to assume that you know what others are thinking about you or some aspect of your performance. Rather than acknowledging that it is impossible to know for certain the content of another person's mind, you believe that their assumptions (usually negative) are correct.

5. Labelling

This is about evaluating your whole self on the basis of one or more characteristics, actions or thoughts. It is similar to over-generalisation, or the 'part-whole' error, because an absolute label is given to the whole, based on just one or some of its components. For example, you might label yourself an 'idiot' for making just one mistake.

6. Fortune-telling

This refers to making predictions (usually negative) about the future. This often results in AVOIDANCE and procrastination. Continually predicting negative outcomes can become a self-fulfilling prophecy. For example, a depressed person predicts they will not enjoy playing their usual game of five-a-side football with friends and so avoids doing so. They also predict that they will be unable to cope with their daily workload, which increases the likelihood that they will become overwhelmed should they make a start on the list of tasks.

7. Emotional reasoning

This describes using strong emotions as reliable indicators of reality. This can be problematic as you then cease to seek out alternative information that may provide a more accurate account of a situation. For example, someone with OCD assumes that, because they feel so intensely anxious when they leave the house, they probably left the door unlocked.

8. Personalisation

This describes the tendency to place yourself at the centre of negative events. Rather than taking into account other contributing factors, you assume personal responsibility for an undesirable outcome. For example, you notice your partner appears irritable and aloof and automatically assume you have done something to displease them.

9. Magnification and minimisation

This refers to ATTENTIONAL BIAS, where a person tends to focus on negative features of themselves or a situation, and magnify their severity, while ignoring or minimising positive features. For example, during a pleasant night out with friends, you mistake the name of one of your friends' partners. At home that evening, you ruminate on how much offence you must have caused, even though you have no evidence to suggest anyone was offended and you have been invited to go out with the group again.

10. Demanding

This is about when you apply rigid rules to yourself, others and the world. These unrelenting rules typically start off as strong preferences and are transmuted into 'should', 'must' and 'have to' imperatives. They leave no room for deviation or error and, when unmet, result in emotional disturbance. For example, because you strongly prefer that people are considerate drivers, you expect everyone always to be a considerate driver.

11. Disqualifying the positive

This describes an information-processing bias similar to mental filtering. The distinction is that, in this case, information that contradicts a strongly held negative belief (such as being unlikable) is disqualified or discounted. Information may also be transmuted to fit with the pre-existing belief. For example, even though you believe yourself to be unlikable, you have a pleasant conversation with a stranger at a party but you subsequently twist this and tell yourself the person you were speaking to was just being polite and couldn't wait to get away from you.

12. Jumping to conclusions

As the name implies, this describes the tendency to leap to a negative interpretation of an event despite the absence of evidence to support it. For example, your partner is late home and you immediately interpret this to mean she's been knocked down by a car while walking home.

Everyone makes thinking errors occasionally. Some you probably make more often than others. COGNITIVE distortions are commonplace and do not indicate psychological or emotional disturbance. They do, however, feature prominently in skewing interpretations of individual experience and hence are clinically informative.

Negative automatic thoughts (NATs)

NEGATIVE AUTOMATIC THOUGHTS (NATS) are thoughts that just seem to pop into your head in certain situations. Frequently these thoughts take the form of truncated sentences such as 'No one likes me'. Typically, NATS are a by-product of the COGNITIVE distortions listed above and are AFFECT LADEN. Automatic thoughts most closely related to an individual's emotional experience are considered to be the most therapeutically relevant and are targeted in CBT treatment (Padesky & Greenberger, 2020).

Because they are seemingly spontaneous and readily accessible to the client, NATS are described as 'automatic'. More accurately, however, NATS arise when assumptions and CORE BELIEFS, which the client may be far less aware of, are triggered.

> **Illustrative example**
> Jamie was a bright child and succeeded at most academic endeavours but he was bullied at school due to being the shortest boy in the class. His parents, in particular his father, placed a high value on athletic ability and teased him for not being good at sports. Regardless of how well he achieved academically at school, he was aware of his father's disappointment that he did not excel at sports. This continued throughout his time at secondary school. When he showed distress about this to his parents, he was told to 'man up'. Jamie developed an image of himself as weak and inadequate and other people as critical and harsh. Despite becoming a successful electrical engineer with a well-paid job, and being only slightly below average height, he was reluctant to pursue a romantic relationship. He would spend an excessive amount of time in the gym and was very concerned and sensitive to comments about his height or physique.

We can see how the negative beliefs that Jamie developed about himself and others in his early life continue to dog him in his adult life.

We can further understand from Jamie's example that CORE BELIEFS (see section below), such as 'I'm inadequate', skew one's interpretation of actual events at A in the ABC MODEL and influence the evaluation assigned to these events at B.

Assumptions

Assumptions are like contingency plans that individuals devise to compensate for their negative CORE BELIEFS. They are another layer of rules that often take the form of 'if–then' statements: for example, 'If I can get others to like me, then I can view myself as a bit worthwhile.' On the other side of the coin, they also act to reinforce the negative CORE BELIEF: for example, 'If I am rejected, then it proves that I am worthless.'

Core beliefs

Long-held beliefs about yourself, other people and the world/life are called CORE BELIEFS or CORE SCHEMATA. They comprise the deepest level of COGNITION and so are not as often at the forefront of people's minds as assumptions and automatic thoughts. They are, however, hardwired into our way of thinking and determine how we make sense of our experiences. CORE BELIEFS are absolute rigid rules that give rise to assumptions and automatic thoughts. They are typically experienced as facts rather than personal beliefs. MALADAPTIVE or unhealthy CORE BELIEFS often lead to emotional and psychological problems that impede goal attainment. Below is an example of the three types of unhealthy CORE BELIEFS:

Self: I'm worthless.
Others: People are cruel.
World/life: Life is perilous.

CORE BELIEFS tend to be formed in childhood and early adult life. Frequently they are formed in response to early experiences. Thus, CORE BELIEFS may well 'fit' with an individual's early understanding of themselves and their world. They also may have served a functional purpose at one time. For example, if you had neglectful and abusive parents, and you were the target of frequent criticism from your teachers, and you also found it difficult to make friends and were subjected to bullying at school, it makes sense that you might conclude (erroneously) that you're worthless. Certainly that message has been consistently received. Your survival instincts may also lead you to conclude that other people are cruel and best treated with suspicion. A further conclusion may be that life itself is harsh and unyielding.

Because CORE BELIEFS are – as the name implies – at the very core of our understanding of ourselves, they are notoriously difficult to shift. An individual will live their life according to the SUBJECTIVE truth of these beliefs. Experiential evidence that contradicts CORE BELIEFS will be ignored, overlooked and misinterpreted. Padesky (1993) equates this information-processing bias with holding a prejudice. Only information consistent with the pre-existent belief system is acknowledged. As a result, CORE SCHEMATA are rarely challenged, re-evaluated or updated by the client. CBT aims to assist clients in reassessing the validity of their unhealthy CORE BELIEFS and to form healthy alternatives.

It is also useful to consider the effects each type of belief (self, other and world) has on the others. To understand more fully an individual's emotional problems, it helps to have a full picture of all three types of CORE BELIEFS they hold. CORE BELIEFS are mutually influential. If a client believes themself to be weak, others to be superior and the world to be unfriendly, it is hardly surprising that they will feel helpless and depressed.

Figure 3.1: The three types of core belief

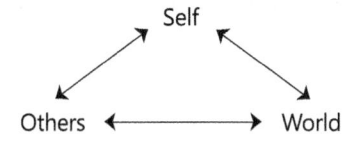

```
           Self
          ↗   ↖
         ↙     ↘
    Others ←——→ World
```

Figure 3.2: The cognitive dartboard

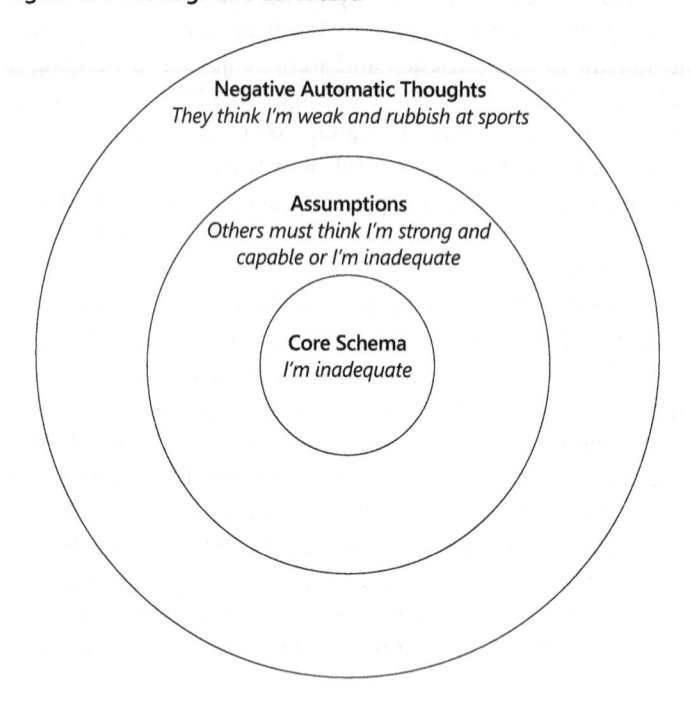

- **Negative Automatic Thoughts**
  They think I'm weak and rubbish at sports
- **Assumptions**
  Others must think I'm strong and capable or I'm inadequate
- **Core Schema**
  I'm inadequate

As Figure 3.2 illustrates, we can conceptualise CORE SCHEMATA as the bull's eye of the COGNITIVE dartboard, with subsequent thoughts radiating from them.

Interaction

The interaction between these three sets of beliefs provides the basis of the CBT conceptual model. Staying with the example of Jamie, we can observe how his CORE BELIEFS influence his interpretation of events and give rise to NATS, assumptions and problematic emotional/behavioural responses.

Core belief
'I'm inadequate.'

Assumption
'If others think I'm physically weak, then I'm inadequate.'

Trigger event
On a work night out, Jamie is introduced to a female colleague's 6ft 3in male romantic partner.

Negative automatic thought
'They both think I'm weak and not masculine enough.'

Emotional response
Shame and depression.

Behavioural response
Jamie drinks a lot of alcohol at the event and talks a lot about how important his work is to the organisation. He avoids looking at the female colleague and makes casual put-downs of her partner.

This is a typical example of how unhealthy CORE SCHEMATA are maintained and reinforced through the misinterpretation of contradictory information and the collection of confirming information. Also note that Jamie's ego-defensive actions (born of his feelings of shame and depression) are likely to alienate his co-worker. His co-worker may be inclined to withdraw from Jamie, which he may interpret as further rejection and proof of his belief that he is inadequate. A vicious cycle perpetuates. Since CORE SCHEMATA are deeply entrenched and almost impervious to DISPUTATION (certainly in the early stages of CBT treatment), intervention is often first directed toward challenging assumptions and re-evaluating interpretations of events. Behavioural responses are also examined for their utility and alternatives are collaboratively devised to bring about more favourable results. Interventions aimed at these areas are often more readily palatable to clients and serve to obliquely erode negative CORE BELIEFS.

A comprehensive discussion of the techniques used to challenge and restructure negative beliefs like Jamie's is beyond the scope of this book. Basic interventions are described in Chapter 6 and further reading is recommended in Appendix 1. Later we will discuss various methods of identifying client beliefs.

Chapter 4
Cognitive behaviour therapy and the therapeutic alliance

Several psychotherapeutic approaches that preceded CBT regard the relationship between client and therapist as the bedrock of therapeutic change.

It is a common criticism that CBT undervalues or even neglects the CORE CONDITIONS as outlined by Carl Rogers (1957). While it is true that CBT holds a specific stance on the THERAPEUTIC ALLIANCE that is at variance with other types of therapy, it is inaccurate to say that CBT fails to recognise the importance of the CORE CONDITIONS. In fact, many of the ALLIANCE CONCEPTS outlined in PSYCHOANALYTIC and humanistic approaches, such as EMPATHY, warmth, CONGRUENCE, UNCONDITIONAL POSITIVE REGARD and TRANSFERENCE and COUNTERTRANSFERENCE, are represented in CBT theory and readily translatable into CBT practice (Prasko et al., 2010; Safran & Segal, 1990; Wills & Sanders, 1997).

Perhaps the most significant point of divergence between Rogerian counselling and CBT is that Rogers considered the CORE CONDITIONS to be both necessary and sufficient for therapeutic change to occur, while CBT regards the conditions as desirable and necessary but not sufficient on their own to bring about client change (Beck et al., 1979).

Rogers' core conditions

Empathy

CBT holds that accurate EMPATHY is extremely important in order for therapy to be effective. Like other therapeutic approaches, CBT recognises that the client needs not only to feel understood but to actually be understood. CBT pays close attention to the behaviours and behavioural tendencies associated with specific emotions. Thus the CBT therapist can readily convey understanding of how the client feels by referring to how they may be acting or may be inclined to act. Additionally, because certain beliefs and thoughts are thematically consistent with specific emotions, CBT therapists are able to convey both affective EMPATHY and philosophical EMPATHY: namely, the therapist demonstrates understanding of the emotions experienced by the client and of the thoughts that give rise to those feelings.

Warmth

A non-judgemental, approachable demeanour is desirable in a CBT therapist. The ability to convey a degree of professional warmth may be particularly useful with depressed or suicidal clients and those with very poor self-opinion. By 'professional warmth', we mean imparting to your client a sense of being liked and respected while maintaining the clear boundaries of a professional relationship.

There are contraindications to be considered regarding warmth toward clients. Clients who lack self-efficacy can become overly dependent on a warm therapist. Also, negative CORE BELIEFS that spur the client to seek approval from others can be inadvertently reinforced through therapist warmth.

There are also potential confounding issues for the therapist. CBT therapists who are overly warm toward their clients may find it more difficult to be active-directive in treatment. It may be difficult for the therapist to establish their role as 'expert' in early treatment if they are overly focused on being warm.

Sometimes it can be challenging for the therapist to feel warmth toward a client who they don't actually like. In this case, forcing it will almost certainly smack of insincerity. Behaving in a polite, interested manner and seeking supervision is recommended in this instance.

Unconditional positive regard

Rather than prizing each client in the Rogerian sense (Rogers, 1957), CBT therapists practise acceptance toward their clients. Acceptance involves recognising the intrinsic value of each client while acknowledging them as a fallible human being. The client is treated with respect and caring, regardless of any mistakes or misdeeds. This is not to say that the CBT therapist will gloss over self-destructive (or other-destructive) behaviours that the client may disclose.

On the contrary, CBT focuses on helping clients to understand and modify behaviours and thoughts that interfere with reaching therapeutic goals. While the client's faulty ways of thinking and acting will be directly evaluated and challenged, this is done without judging them as a whole person. It takes skill for the therapist to be able to confront a client's MALADAPTIVE beliefs and coping strategies without leading the client to infer personal disapproval. Because CBT is an explicit therapy, the practitioner will often devote time to socialising clients to the model. Educating clients about what they can expect to happen in sessions with regard to direct challenges can reduce the risk of clients feeling negatively judged.

Congruence and genuineness

These conditions are perhaps most obviously represented in the context of collaboration, as discussed in the following section. Suffice to say that CBT does not operate any hidden agendas.

The client is privy to the therapist's musings about what may be perpetuating their problems. Additionally, any early experiences that may have contributed to the formation of dysfunctional beliefs are discussed openly between client and therapist. The therapist takes the role of authoritative expert in the field of psychology and is willing to share knowledge with the client. The client is an expert on their own experiences and hence plays a vital role in providing the information necessary for therapeutic work to begin.

Skilled CBT therapists are consistent in how they respond to their clients. They exhibit genuine reactions but are appropriately sensitive to the potential effect on the client. CBT discourages therapist dishonesty and insincerity. Therefore therapists will ideally avoid offering platitudes, false praise or empty compliments. In these ways, CBT therapists are open, genuine and congruent.

Collaboration

The CBT therapist and client working together in a joint endeavour to resolve the client's difficulties is known as COLLABORATIVE EMPIRICISM. This term refers to the working relationship whereby the client provides the therapist with information and the therapist uses their expertise to help the client challenge unhelpful beliefs and behaviour. Initially, the therapist will take a lead role in structuring sessions; as therapy progresses, the client will be encouraged to take the lead more often. This shift in responsibility for leading treatment is in keeping with the CBT objective of assisting clients to become their own therapists.

Because client and therapist are working together, any hypotheses made by the therapist are offered to the client for confirmation, disconfirmation or adjustment. Additionally, rather than forming silent interpretations, the therapist will explore the client's emotions, thoughts and behaviours overtly. In addition to being a structured, goal-directed treatment, CBT acknowledges that a good working alliance promotes client trust and thereby increases compliance. Because between-session assignments are an integral part of CBT treatment, the client needs to feel that the therapist is genuinely interested in their progress and understands their problems. Otherwise the client is less likely to carry out goal-directed 'homework' tasks, which are often challenging and uncomfortable.

Use of humour

Therapy can be a serious business. Certainly the suffering of those with psychological and emotional disorders is no laughing matter. That said, Albert Ellis, founder of REBT, proposes that individuals with neurotic disorders frequently fall prey to taking themselves and certain life events overly seriously (Dryden & Branch, 2008). The appropriate use of humour may help strengthen the alliance and normalise symptoms and can help to humanise the therapist. When used therapeutically, humour can also encourage the client to take a more light-hearted view of faulty thinking and self-defeating behaviours (see Dionigi & Canestrari (2018) for a discussion on humour in COGNITIVE therapy). The judicial use of humour encourages the client to laugh at aspects of their thinking and actions while simultaneously holding an accepting and compassionate attitude toward themself, rather than berate themself for experiencing emotional problems.

We emphasise that it is not appropriate for the therapist to make jokes at the client's expense or to use humour to ease their own personal discomfort within the session. As with any intervention, humour should be employed for the potential benefit it may hold for the client.

Caution and forethought are recommended when using humour. Some clients may welcome a joke or two but covertly use it to avoid discussing painful emotions or to deflect the therapist from more serious dimensions of the therapy. Clients with CORE BELIEFS about needing to be liked and approved of may use humour as a way of 'winning over' the therapist. It is worth paying close attention to signs that your client is making it their job to keep you entertained in sessions.

Therapist self-disclosure

Unlike other schools of psychotherapy, CBT supports the prudent use of therapist self-disclosure. When patients ask the therapist questions, they will frequently benefit from an honest and measured answer. After all, CBT is a collaborative process and it follows that the exchange of information is, to a degree, two-way. Certainly questions pertaining to the therapist's training or experience of working with a specific problem area are well within the client's right to ask. CBT therapists will answer such questions honestly and responsibly.

Clients may also pose a host of different questions to the therapist, particularly once it has been established that it is acceptable to do so. Some of these questions may be inconsequential and asked out of politeness or common curiosity, such as 'Where are you going on holiday this summer?' or 'Did you have a nice weekend?' With these types of questions, there is little risk to consider, and brief, polite responses will normally suffice. At other times, the client may ask more personal questions based on whatever is being discussed in session. Forthright questions such as 'Are you divorced?' and more obliquely phrased ones such as, 'I don't know, perhaps you've been through a divorce yourself...' require thoughtful handling. The general rule is to answer questions if doing so is likely to be helpful, or at least not harmful, for the client. Questions of a personal nature can be awkward for therapists. Some therapists are able to answer such enquiries while maintaining a professional stance. Others may choose not to answer but will provide the client with a reasonable explanation for their refusal.

In certain instances, the therapist may also choose to disclose unsolicited information. Telling anecdotes, using metaphors and sharing stories related to your client's situation might benefit the alliance, instil hope of recovery or provide a useful template for understanding problems.

It is always important to assess the possible effect of sharing personal information with your client. Ask yourself:

- How is my client likely to make sense of this information?
- Will giving this information impact negatively on the THERAPEUTIC ALLIANCE?
- Will my client be able to use this information constructively?

Transference and countertransference

These concepts comprise much of analytical therapeutic approaches. While CBT does not incorporate TRANSFERENCE as a key aspect of therapeutic intervention, it does acknowledge the role it plays in the therapeutic relationship. Just as every client brings to the session their own belief systems, so do therapists.

First, the client may wittingly or unwittingly attempt to elicit responses from the therapist that are in keeping with their CORE SCHEMATA. In this sense, the client engages in 'schema maintenance' (Young et al., 2003), which is similar to TRANSFERENCE. In essence, the client provokes in the therapist the type of reaction they expect to receive from others. Unlike traditional psychoanalysts, the CBT practitioner may well discuss this phenomenon openly with the client, when it is deemed timely and appropriate.

Second, therapist reactions to the client and/or the material shared are considered within the context of the therapist's idiosyncratic belief system. Hence the therapist is responsible for their own emotional responses to the client. This notion is not entirely dissimilar to COUNTERTRANSFERENCE. To clarify, client and therapist schemata can often bump up against one another and produce complex nuances in the alliance. The CBT therapist's personal reactions to the client will be discussed and conceptualised, as per the ABC MODEL, in supervision.

In conclusion

Because of its scientific basis and structured approach, CBT can be difficult to master while adhering to Rogers' CORE CONDITIONS (1957). Students and trainees often seem to be so focused on getting the treatment sequence correct that adherence to the CORE CONDITIONS temporarily seems to fly out of the consulting room window. Maintaining the CORE CONDITIONS while conducting competent CBT takes practice and is an issue frequently addressed in trainee supervision.

Despite comparatively sparse mention of the CORE CONDITIONS in much of CBT literature, they are a key feature of CBT's overall approach. Gilbert and Leahy (2007) have helped fill this gap through their writings on the role of the therapeutic relationship in CBT. Rather than being guilty of neglecting or rejecting the importance of the THERAPEUTIC ALLIANCE, perhaps it is more accurate to say that CBT has fallen foul of taking it for granted. CBT may benefit from further disseminating its unique viewpoint on the conditions that favourably influence therapeutic change. Fortunately, more research is currently focused on this area: for example, Moorey and Lavender (2019) discuss this in detail, and hopefully texts such as this book will help to dispel accusations of CBT as insensitive to the relationship between therapist and client.

Chapter 5
Case conceptualisation

Basic conceptualisation

CASE CONCEPTUALISATION, sometimes referred to as case formulation, is a means of understanding the client's main presenting problems. It describes the client's symptoms, disorders and current problem(s). Conceptualisations come in two forms: longitudinal formulations, sometimes referred to as generic formulations, and disorder-specific formulations.

Padesky and Mooney (1990) developed a generic model sometimes referred to as the 'hot cross bun' because of its appearance (see Figure 5.1). This model pulls together environmental, COGNITIVE, behavioural and biological factors, showing how these impact on one another. While this is not a longitudinal formulation, it provides a useful, simple overview that can help clients see their problems as multidimensional and serves to psycho-educate the client on the separate components (COGNITION, emotion, behaviour, physiology). As Wills and Sanders (1997) point out, this model can be very useful for clients who attribute their difficulties wholly to biological and medical factors. Because it includes all aspects of the client's functioning, it serves as a palatable introduction to a psychological perspective on human disturbance.

Case conceptualisation 45

Figure 5.1: Hot cross bun (simplified model) (Padesky & Mooney, 1990)

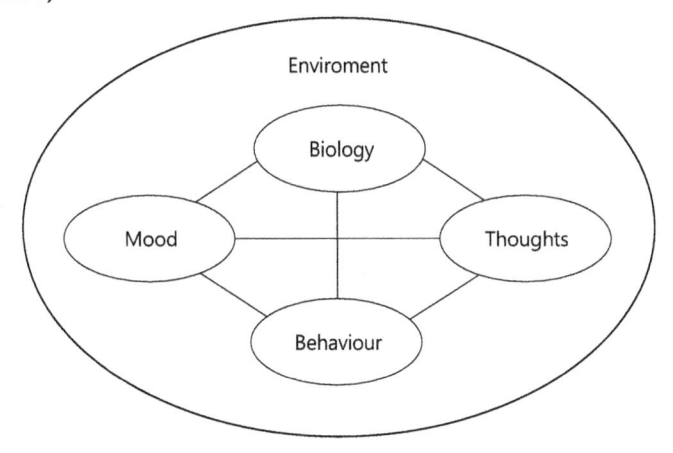

Figure 5.2: Simple vicious flower demonstrating how illness anxiety is maintained (adapted from Hackman, 1998)

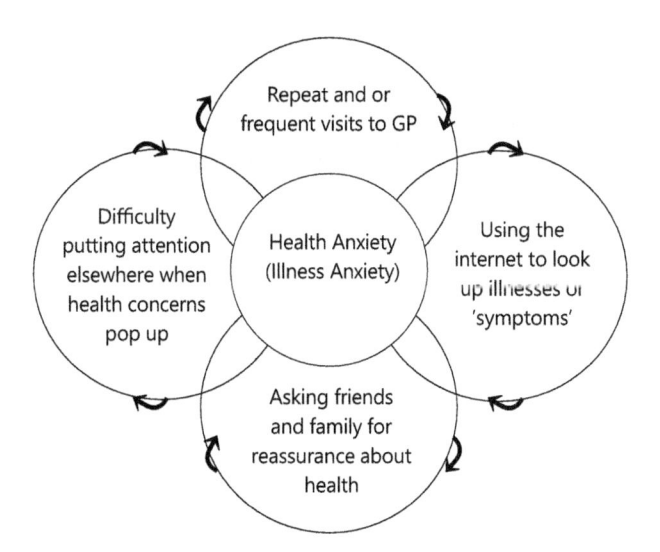

Another simple but effective conceptualisation tool is the 'vicious flower' (Hackman, 1998) (Figure 5.2). This model exhibits how the client's main problem produces symptoms (thoughts and behaviours) that, in turn, further reinforce and maintain the primary problem. This model is of particular use when treating ANXIETY disorders, because of the tendency for sufferers to use AVOIDANCE strategies that prevent them from confronting their fears. A further advantage of the vicious flower is that as many petals as necessary can be added on.

The vicious flower has been developed to give a fuller view of problem causation and maintenance (Figure 5.3).

Figure 5.3: Detailed vicious flower

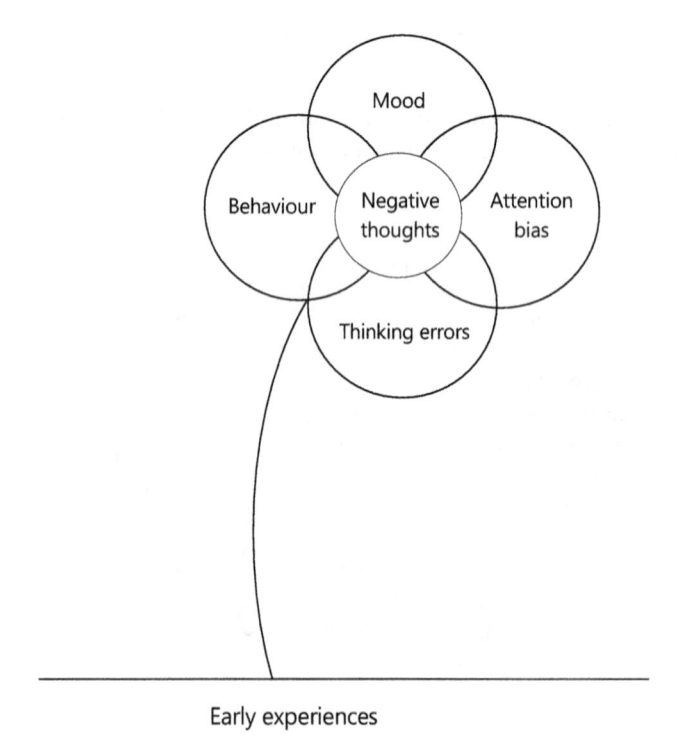

Early experiences

Detailed conceptualisation

A generic/longitudinal formulation sets out the mechanisms (i.e. dysfunctional beliefs and behaviours) that the therapist proposes may be influencing the client's current problems, and also includes relevant (typically) early experiences that are thought to have played a part in the development of the mechanisms (beliefs/behaviours). An example of a longitudinal formulation can be seen in Dryden and Branch (2012). Formulations often contain diagrammatic cycles (maintenance cycles) that illustrate how different aspects of the formulation affect and maintain the problem (Figure 5.4).

Figure 5.4: Diagrammatic maintenance cycle

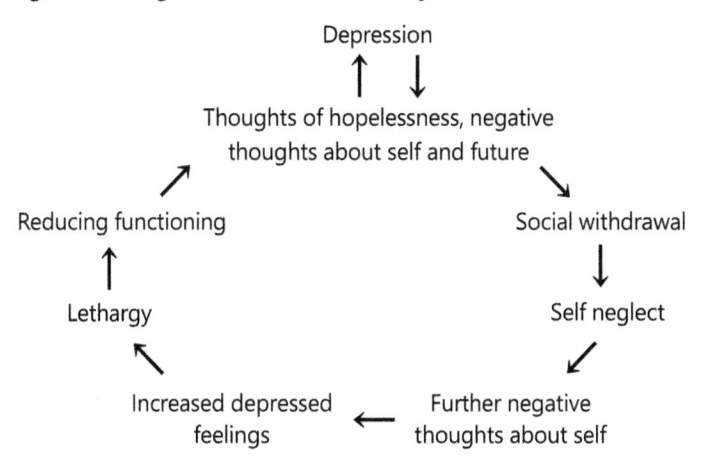

```
                    Depression
                      ↑   ↓
         Thoughts of hopelessness, negative
            thoughts about self and future
           ↗                              ↘
Reducing functioning                      Social withdrawal
     ↑                                          ↓
  Lethargy                                  Self neglect
     ↖                                        ↙
        Increased depressed    ←    Further negative
            feelings                  thoughts about self
```

A simple conceptualisation is enough to be getting on with. Generally represented in ABC FORMAT, it serves to identify TRIGGER EVENTS (A); thoughts, evaluations and assumptions (B); plus emotional, behavioural and COGNITIVE responses (C). As problems are worked through, themes may begin to emerge that indicate the presence of CORE SCHEMATA. Therefore, as therapy progresses and more information about the client is gathered, conceptualisation develops more fully. The CBT therapist keeps an eye on underlying mechanisms that may be maintaining problems and considers historical experiences that may have contributed to the formation of unhelpful CORE BELIEFS. As always, the development of a detailed conceptualisation includes input from both the client and therapist.

The process of deepening and refining the overall picture of the client's problems can help to strengthen client understanding of how they have arrived where they are today. This increased insight may help the client to better recognise potential points for intervention. It also provides a bridge between past and present experiences (Wills & Sanders, 1997).

> **Illustrative example**
>
> Georgia suffers from depression and anxiety. Although she is performing well at work, she often worries that her employment contract will not be renewed, despite good feedback from her managers. She spends most of her weekends preparing work for the coming week. She spends little time on leisure activities and feels exhausted most days. She often cancels or cuts short time with friends because she doesn't see it as the most effective way to spend her time, but then feels guilty and thinks she is a bad friend. She has trouble turning down work tasks and, as a result, has a much heavier workload than colleagues in the same role. She gets very anxious about performing at work in front of colleagues. Georgia's parents are of the Windrush generation and built a life in the UK from nothing. They raised Georgia with a strong work ethic and all her life have encouraged and validated working hard and personal sacrifice. They are now retired and have returned to the Caribbean.

Using the information in this example, we can build a comprehensive conceptualisation of Georgia's current problems of depression and ANXIETY. (The conceptualisation format is adapted from Judith Beck (2011).)

Presenting problems
Depression
Performance ANXIETY and general worry

Significant early/childhood experiences
Mum worked when Georgia was growing up, while also keeping house. Father also worked long hours and spent little time with the family.

Environmental factors
Living alone (rented flat).
Minimal contact with family as they live in another country.
Temporary employment contract in a competitive profession.

Core beliefs
Self: I'm not good enough.
Others: Others are critical and judgemental.
World: Life favours the strong.

Assumptions/rules
If I am criticised, it proves I am not good enough.
I must always work hard to make up for not being good enough.
As long as I am viewed as competent, then I am good enough.

Activating events
Any kind of feedback at work that is less than 100% positive, even if intended as constructive critical comment.
Making simple errors at work.

Compensatory strategies
Assumes others are critical until proven otherwise.
Backs down in confrontations.
Works hard to please others and avoid criticism.

Disorder-specific formulations

In addition to developing a longitudinal formulation, CBT therapists will often make use of a disorder-specific formulation. These are COGNITIVE behavioural models that demonstrate what mechanisms (i.e. beliefs/NATs/behaviours) are most relevant to a particular disorder (i.e. panic disorder). They make use of diagnostic criteria (for example, *DSM-5* (APA, 2013), or *ICD-10* (WHO, 1990)) and provide a COGNITIVE behavioural explanation for the problem/disorder.

Many COGNITIVE models (disorder-specific formulations) for common mental health disorders, such as depression (Beck et al., 1979), OBSESSIVE-COMPULSIVE DISORDER (OCD) (Salkovskis, 1985), panic disorder (Clark, 1986) and social ANXIETY (Hope et al., 2010), have been developed and refined since the 1970s. Each model demonstrates key diagnostic features, specific COGNITIVE themes and typical behaviours and associated affect that are commonly presented by people with the disorder. For example, the COGNITIVE model of panic (Clark, 1986) demonstrates how the misinterpretation of physical symptoms (COGNITION) leads to increased ANXIETY (emotion), which increases panic sensations (physiology), which can then lead to a panic attack. In order to avoid the panic attack, people typically avoid the situation (behaviour), or engage in SAFETY BEHAVIOURS to prevent the feared outcome. For a detailed exploration of disorder-specific formulations, see Tarrier & Johnson (2016).

Considerations when forming a conceptualisation

A conceptualisation is like a road map that is intended to help both client and therapist arrive at a particular destination. It helps therapist and client to tackle problems in a sensible order, thereby directing treatment toward therapeutic goals. A well-constructed problem formulation can be invaluable as it makes clear the most advantageous areas at which to target interventions and provides information about which techniques are most likely to be of benefit. Trainees and experienced therapists alike find that presenting CASE CONCEPTUALISATIONS helps them to make good use of clinical supervision.

It is important to remember, however, that every therapist brings their own clinical experience and theoretical knowledge to their conceptualisation. Clients are idiosyncratic individuals, even though their emotional disturbances may be very well documented and familiar to the therapist. Hence, it cannot be stressed enough that the client should be included in the process of building a conceptualisation. Not every client will fit as neatly into a pre-existing model as may be expected. It pays to listen closely to your client's description of how they experience difficulties and to avoid concluding that they are a 'textbook' case. The client should ideally be given regular opportunities to disagree with, subtly adjust or entirely reject the formulation. Often clients are reluctant to voice objections to the therapist, for a host of reasons, and need to be directly encouraged to do so. It is the therapist's task to form a good working alliance with their clients and to be clear that CBT is a two-person therapy. The therapist may be the expert in CBT but that does not mean that they are always right. Above all, CBT therapists need to be flexible and modify conceptualisations as new information emerges throughout treatment.

Chapter 6
Cognitive restructuring techniques

The process of assessment in CBT begins to socialise the client to the CBT model. Asking clients to identify ways of thinking in relation to emotional and practical problems introduces the principle of THOUGHT–FEELING INTERACTION. Sometimes just asking the client to be more mindful of their thoughts, beliefs and personal rules for living can be enough to kickstart COGNITIVE modification. However, to effect meaningful, long-lasting change to entrenched personal schema, much diligent practice is required. COGNITIVE RESTRUCTURING takes place at any level of COGNITION, although changes are more philosophically profound and pervasive when they occur at core schema level.

For every negative schema challenged and eroded, a healthy alternative schema needs to be developed and strengthened. The same applies for interpretations, NEGATIVE AUTOMATIC THOUGHTS (NATs) and assumptions. We offer some examples below.

Core belief (negative): I'm unlovable.
Healthy alternative: I'm lovable.

Assumption (negative): I must be in a relationship to be lovable. If I'm not in a relationship, it means I am unlovable.
Healthy alternative: I am lovable regardless of whether I am being actively loved.

Negative automatic thought: Sandra isn't interested in me because I'm so rubbish.
Healthy alternative: I can't be romantically interesting to all people, as much as I'd like that to be true.

Interpretation (negative): My date isn't very talkative because they are not interested in pursuing a relationship with me.
Healthy alternative: There are many reasons why my date may not be very talkative, and it may be nothing to do with them not being interested.

In this chapter we will look at some of the more common methods of challenging dysfunctional thoughts and strengthening healthy alternative ways of thinking.

In order to begin work on restructuring thoughts, the client first needs to be prepared to do a few things. They need to:

- understand and accept the psychological component of their problems. In short, thoughts and feelings are closely linked, therefore dysfunctional thinking leads to emotional disturbance
- become more aware of their thinking in general, and specifically in relation to their identified problems
- catch and record NATs, thinking distortions and assumptions in TRIGGER situations
- develop a willingness to be sceptical about the validity of their thoughts and beliefs.

It is the therapist's task to help the client achieve these. They may use techniques such as teaching examples, metaphors, DIDACTIC explanation, bibliotherapy and SOCRATIC QUESTIONING.

Daily thought records

The daily thought record (DTR) is perhaps one of the forms most frequently used in early sessions of CBT. It has its uses throughout treatment but is probably most useful when clients are just beginning to relate their thoughts to their emotions. Many different versions of the thought record exist. Some

Figure 6.1: Daily thought record

Date	EMOTION(S)	SITUATION	AUTOMATIC THOUGHTS	THINKING ERRORS YOU ARE ENGAGING IN	RATIONAL RESPONSE	OUTCOME RE-RATE MOOD NOW (0–100)
	What do you feel? How bad is it? (0–100)	What were you doing? Where were you?	What exactly were your thoughts? How far did you believe each of them? (0–100)		What are your rational answers to the automatic thoughts? How much do you believe each of them?	How much do you believe original thoughts? (0–100) What can you do now?

are simpler and omit headings included on the traditional DTR. The traditional DTR (see Figure 6.1) has the benefit of providing space to identify TRIGGER situations, NATs, thinking errors, healthy alternative thoughts and resulting emotions all on one page. (Unfortunately this comprehensive format leaves much less space for the client to write in, which is a drawback.) The DTR is generally given to the client to use between sessions and bring back to the therapist for collaborative review.

ABC forms

Like the DTR, many different versions of the ABC form (Figure 6.2) are available. They can be used as an assessment tool or instead of a DTR. The form itself is pretty self-explanatory. It is used to break down the client's problem into three distinct components: a definite TRIGGER, thought and emotion. CBT therapists often give their clients ABC forms to use between sessions and will go over them with the client in the next session. A single form is used for each specific example of a target problem.

Figure 6.2: ABC form

ABC form

A (ACTIVATING EVENT)
  What happened?
  Where were you?
  When was it?

B (BELIEFS)
  What thoughts did you have about the event?

C (CONSEQUENCES)
  Emotional
  How did you feel?
  What emotion did you experience?

  Behavioural
  What did you do?
  What did you feel inclined to do?

Recording challenges to negative thinking

DISPUTING negative beliefs in session is extremely useful. Because clients believe so firmly in their view of things, it is frequently difficult for them to generate convincing arguments against their negative thoughts. For this reason, the CBT therapist will typically do the bulk of the DISPUTING in the first instance. Once the client has grasped the process, they are encouraged to form their own DISPUTES. The purpose of challenging negative thoughts is (rather obviously) to promote psychological health through the formation of more ADAPTIVE belief systems. By developing arguments 'for' a new belief and 'against' an old one, the client begins to truly embrace positive change. These arguments then need to be repeated by the client between sessions. Simply telling the client to think x instead of y does not bring about profound belief change. Rather, the therapist shows the client how to use challenges to increase their strength of belief in new ways of thinking. The next section describes different types of questions that both client and therapist can use to this end. Recording challenges, either by writing them down or taping the therapy session, helps the client to remember useful points.

Questions

The liberal use of questions encourages the client to work things out for themself. It is generally accepted that people retain information better when they have been actively involved in the process of gathering it. All the questions used in DISPUTING are intended to help the client realise these three points:

- Negative beliefs are not evidentially supported. They are not provable and hence are not facts.
- Negative beliefs impede problem-solving. Faulty thinking impairs functioning.
- Negative beliefs produce unpleasant, disproportionate emotional responses to negative events.

The following example questions can be used to both challenge negative beliefs and support newer, positive beliefs:

- What evidence do you have to support this belief?
- What proof can you give to support this belief?
- How does thinking this way lead you to behave?
- Is there any additional information you might be overlooking?
- Can you think of an alternative explanation for what happened?
- How is holding this belief helping you to reach your goals?
- If someone you really cared about held this belief, what would you say to them?
- Would you recommend this way of thinking to a friend? If not, why not?
- How does thinking in this way leave you feeling?
- What would be a more constructive way of thinking about the situation?
- What effect does this way of thinking have on your overall mood?
- Although you strongly feel this belief to be true, can you entertain the possibility that you may be wrong?

Role-play

Role-play is an effective means of reinforcing belief change. The therapist pretends to hold the client's negative beliefs and the client gets the opportunity to play therapist. By using arguments to convince the therapist to doubt their pretend negative beliefs and generate better alternatives, the client is effectively challenging their own beliefs. This is a core CBT skill that therapists strive to impart to clients. It is important to get the balance right between making it too easy or too difficult for the client to sway your thinking. Taking a step back from their own beliefs via role-play can help the client understand just how unproductive and even ridiculous some of their thinking is.

Role-play can also be used to help clients rehearse acting in a new way. Unassertive clients often benefit from role-playing confrontational situations with their therapist in preparation for a real event.

Old meaning–new meaning

CORE SCHEMATA are notoriously intractable, so it is good practice to use more than one strategy to shift them. Since negative CORE BELIEFS are usually developed in early life, they are typically formed as a result of certain types of unfavourable experiences. The meanings we attach to these early events are the essence of the beliefs we ultimately adopt. If meanings given to early experiences are not updated, then negative beliefs formed at the time will continue to inform our understanding of others, the world and ourselves.

The old meaning–new meaning technique is intended to help the client revisit formative experiences and reassess assigned meanings from their current, more mature and better-informed perspective. This exercise may need to be repeated several times in order to truly root out ancient CORE BELIEFS. It is often used in session to give the client the added support of the therapist's guidance and input. It can be used as a homework assignment but it is imperative that the therapist allots sufficient time in sessions to reviewing and 'tweaking' the client's work. CORE SCHEMATA are customarily challenged in mid-stage treatment once the alliance has been established and more superficial COGNITIONS have been confronted. In some cases, however, CORE BELIEFS are articulated fully in early sessions and can be tackled (with skill and professional sensitivity) straight away.

Illustrative example

Stephen's dad found it difficult to control his anger. He was quick to temper and was frequently verbally and physically aggressive. His aggressive outbursts were even more intense when he drank, which he often did. Stephen remembers feeling frequently anxious and apprehensive about his father returning home from work in the evenings. He tried desperately to develop a bond with his father, but this was often rejected or responded to with cruelty. Stephen remembers an incident when he was 10 years old, when his father promised him a new video game if he behaved well. He did everything he was told, and his father took him took him to the video game shop, only to tell him when they were in the shop that he didn't deserve a game, and they left the shop with nothing. Stephen's mother did little to protect him from his father's outbursts and would usually tell him to 'just stay out the way'. Stephen developed the belief that 'other people are not to be trusted', and that he was 'a burden and ultimately worthless'.

Figure 6.3 is a worked through 'old meaning–new meaning' form based on this example.

Figure 6.3: Old meaning–new meaning form

EVENT	OLD MEANING	NEW MEANING
What happened? When? Who was involved?	What did it mean to you (or about you) at the time?	What is a more accurate meaning you can assign the event now?
1. Age 6, I fell and cut my lip open. I got blood on my dad's shirt and he yelled at me and sent me away.	1. I should have been careful and not run around the house, like I was told. Because I made the mistake, I didn't deserve care.	1. Children make mistakes and parents should care for them regardless. I should have been cleaned up and looked after.
2. Age 9, I was due to be picked up from an after-school club I insisted on going to. My parents forgot to pick me up.	2. I shouldn't want things that inconvenience other people. I'm a burden and not worth picking up.	2. Although the club meant my home time differed from normal, my parents should have made a note and picked me up to keep me safe.

| 3. Age 11, I left a toy in the hallway and dad tripped and fell on it. He hit me around the head and mum told me I shouldn't leave toys out. | 3. It's my fault dad gets angry and hits me. I deserve it. | 3. Children make a mess and parents can deal with this without resorting to violence. I didn't deserve to be hit in the face. I wasn't the problem; my dad had an anger problem. |

Ascribing new meanings to old events is a powerful therapeutic experience for many clients. However, very few clients will notice an immediate positive effect on their emotions. It's as though there is a time lag between COGNITIVE RESTRUCTURING and improved mood. Although they are mediated by COGNITION, emotions take a while to 'catch up' with altered thinking. It takes time (and effort) for intellectual insight to impact on emotions. Dryden and Branch (2008) refer to this treatment stage, when the client knows a healthy belief is true but does not yet feel that it is true, as the 'head–gut' issue.

Emotions are a visceral experience. Unhealthy negative emotions seem to leave behind an affective residue. Hence behavioural reinforcement is essential for improved thinking to translate to improved mood. CBT therapists will ideally take care to explain this phenomenon to their clients.

Acting 'as if'

When a client understands a new belief to be true and helpful but does not yet feel it to be true in their gut, the 'as-if' exercise is very useful. It works on the principle that acting in line with a belief serves to reinforce that way of thinking. It is difficult and uncomfortable for people to act in a way that contradicts a strongly held belief. The psychological term for this is COGNITIVE DISSONANCE. In order to reduce the discomfort experienced by COGNITIVE DISSONANCE, people will either make their behaviour consistent with their beliefs or modify their beliefs so that they are consistent with their actions.

For example, Arun believes that he is boring and unlikable and that, if he attempts to engage with others socially, he is likely to be rejected. Arun is encouraged by his therapist to go into a social situation acting as if he truly believes that he is a likeable person. Arun goes to a creative writing group at his university and makes eye contact with other members, sits among them, makes small talk and maintains open, non-defensive body posture. Through manifesting the behaviours of someone who thinks of themselves as likeable, Arun begins to experience COGNITIVE DISSONANCE. The inconsistency between his negative self-opinion and his socially confident behaviour forces him to re-evaluate his belief. Arun also gets a chance to gather information that disproves his prediction that he will be rejected if he makes a social effort.

Imagery work

Imagery is used in several different ways in CBT treatment. Two of the many possible ways imagery can be used include:

- The client is asked to imagine holding a healthy belief with the aim of making the belief more 'real' to them. They are asked to imagine how their behaviour would be different if they were living with this new way of thinking. They may also be asked to imagine specific benefits arising from a changed belief.
- The client is asked to imagine a typical, vivid or recent example of a TRIGGER situation. The therapist encourages the client to imagine being in that same situation but with their new, improved way of thinking. The idea is that the client will experience some degree of emotional change and/or be able to imagine using coping strategies effectively.

Negative mental images are a maintaining feature of several of the ANXIETY disorders. CBT therapists may get the client to change the outcome of catastrophic images. For example, they may help the client to visualise a more positive outcome whereby they cope with a difficult situation more effectively.

People suffering from OBSESSIVE-COMPULSIVE DISORDER (OCD) frequently experience distressing intrusive mental images (Veale & Willson, 2005). The mental images (although unwelcome) are not themselves the problem. Rather, it is the degree of emotional disturbance the client experiences in response to intrusive images that is the problem. OCD sufferers typically assign faulty meanings to intrusive thoughts and images, such as 'Normal people don't get these thoughts' or 'Having these images pop into my head means that I'm bad and dangerous'. With this client population, CBT treatment involves helping the client accept the presence of unwanted mental activity and reassign more benign meanings to unpleasant images.

CBT recognises the value in probing clients about images accompanying negative emotional states. Clients often neglect to report strong or recurrent images to the therapist. This may often be due to embarrassment, shame or simply not understanding that images are of clinical relevance.

The COGNITIVE techniques included in this chapter are by no means exhaustive. For more information, refer to the recommended reading in Appendix 1 and the sources listed in the references.

Zig-zag technique

The zig-zag technique (see Figure 6.4) can be used to strengthen a healthy alternative. A therapist can do this with the client, in a form of role-play, but over time the aim is for the client to become proficient at noticing an unhealthy belief, constructing an alternative and fighting hard to argue for it. First, the client is invited to identify a belief that they want to strengthen, and to rate how strongly they currently believe it (0–100%). In the next box, the client writes down all their doubts and reservations about the healthy belief. In the next box they record any counter-arguments to these doubts and reservations and try to defend the healthy belief. This exercise is continued until they have gone through and exhausted all the attacks on the healthy belief. Finally, the client again rates the strength of their healthy belief, from 1–100%, to assess any shift towards believing it.

Figure 6.4: The zig-zag technique

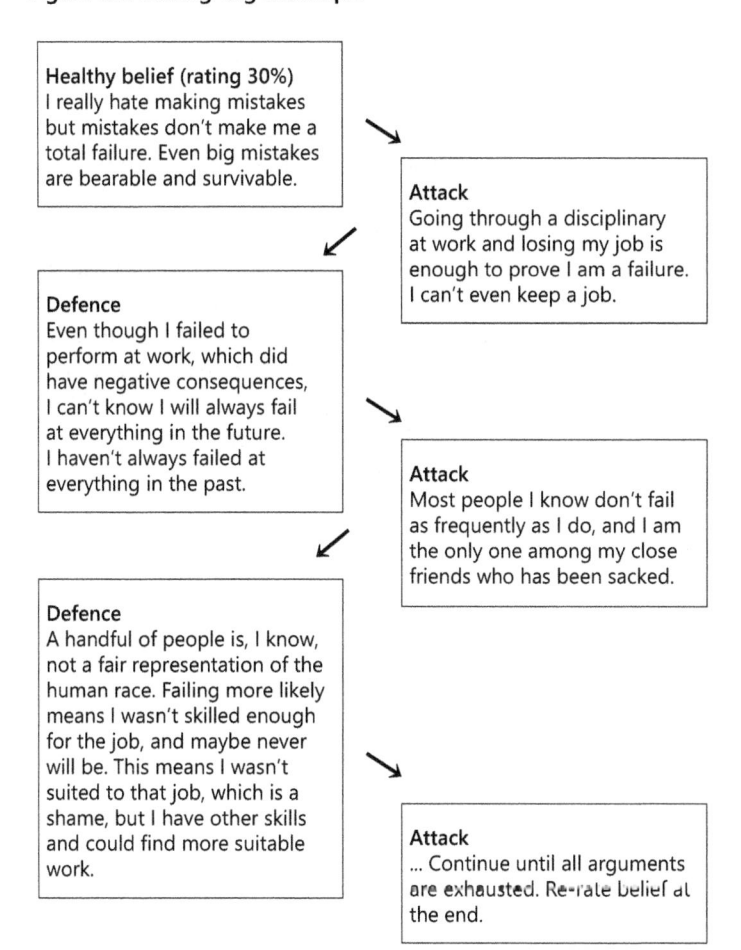

Healthy belief (rating 30%)
I really hate making mistakes but mistakes don't make me a total failure. Even big mistakes are bearable and survivable.

Attack
Going through a disciplinary at work and losing my job is enough to prove I am a failure. I can't even keep a job.

Defence
Even though I failed to perform at work, which did have negative consequences, I can't know I will always fail at everything in the future. I haven't always failed at everything in the past.

Attack
Most people I know don't fail as frequently as I do, and I am the only one among my close friends who has been sacked.

Defence
A handful of people is, I know, not a fair representation of the human race. Failing more likely means I wasn't skilled enough for the job, and maybe never will be. This means I wasn't suited to that job, which is a shame, but I have other skills and could find more suitable work.

Attack
... Continue until all arguments are exhausted. Re-rate belief at the end.

Best friend tactic

When helping clients to hold more helpful, functional beliefs, it can be useful to ask them to consider how someone close to them might view the situation/themselves. It is important to select a person whose opinion the client values, and this is often a best friend. This technique enables the therapist to guide the client to a fairer and more compassionate alternative belief. The alternative belief can be how the client assumes the best friend would view the client, or how the client would view the best friend if they held this dysfunctional belief.

For example, the client believes: 'Because my partner doesn't love me any more, I am unlovable.' The therapist will then ask the client if any of their friends have experienced a similar situation, and say: 'Do you also believe that, because your friend is currently single, they are unlovable? If not why not?' Once the therapist and client have come up with reasons why the best friend is still lovable despite being single, the therapist can use this information to highlight a double standard (a rule the client holds for others but not for themself). To further reinforce this, the pros and cons of holding the new functional/healthy belief and acting in accordance with it can also be discussed and built into between-session tasks/homework assignments.

Chapter 7
Behavioural techniques

Behavioural techniques feature prominently in CBT treatment for almost any type of psychological problem. Although considerable emphasis is placed on the MALADAPTIVE effects of faulty COGNITION in CBT theory, in actual practice it is often more expedient to begin treatment with behavioural interventions. In cases of severe depression, for example, COGNITIVE change is often best achieved through behavioural modification, in the first instance (Beck et al., 1979).

As we touched on in Chapter 6, the reinforcing effects of certain behavioural compensatory strategies on negative beliefs and AVERSIVE EMOTIONS are not to be underestimated or ignored. Typically, different types of emotional problems are associated with thematically consistent modes of thought and action. It therefore makes sense to consider these three areas – emotions, thoughts and behaviours – as part of an interactive system, rather than as disparate entities. Targeting interventions at one of these areas is likely to encourage positive change in the other two, and vice versa.

In this chapter we will look at the types of behaviour that maintain and perpetuate common emotional problems, such as ANXIETY, depression and guilt.

We also briefly describe the typical CBT interventions used to target problematic behaviours. Please bear in mind that this chapter is intended to provide a 'taster' or overview of behavioural interventions used in standard CBT treatment and is not a complete guide. We recommend the further reading in Appendix 1, which discusses in detail the specialised CBT treatment protocols for specific disorders. An overview of behavioural activation (BA) is also included, as there is much evidence in support of BA for the treatment of depression.

Safety behaviours

SAFETY BEHAVIOUR is a term used to describe the lengths to which people will go to keep themselves 'safe' from a predicted negative event. This term is particularly used in the assessment and treatment of ANXIETY disorders such as OBSESSIVE-COMPULSIVE DISORDER (OCD), phobias, social ANXIETY, agoraphobia and panic disorder. Because ANXIETY disorders are generally associated with an elevated expectation of imminent danger and a diminished perception of personal capacity to cope with a specific threat or danger, sufferers will develop (sometimes very elaborate) methods of avoiding 'risky' situations and reducing anxious feelings. Unfortunately, these AVOIDANCE strategies (SAFETY BEHAVIOURS) serve to reinforce the idea that danger is around every corner and compound the sufferer's belief that they are unable to cope in ANXIETY-provoking situations. Rather than coming to realise that ANXIETY, while unpleasant, is survivable, the sufferer continues to believe that their SAFETY STRATEGIES are responsible for staving off a catastrophic outcome.

CBT practitioners will carefully investigate the SAFETY BEHAVIOURS the client is using and help them understand the detrimental effect these behaviours ultimately have on overcoming the target problem. In essence, the client will be helped to realise that AVOIDANCE deprives them of the opportunity to experience different, neutral or more positive outcomes from those their ANXIETY predicts. Once this rationale is clear, the client is encouraged to enter situations that typically provoke their ANXIETY without using SAFETY BEHAVIOURS.

Below are some fictional examples of typical SAFETY STRATEGIES associated with social ANXIETY and panic disorder.

Illustrative example

Romy experiences anxiety in group social situations, including when socialising with her close friends. She feels very anxious before she is due to meet them and often rehearses topics of conversation in her head. When with her friends, she avoids putting forward her opinions, for fear her friends will disagree with her or think she is boring or stupid. She worries she will come across as 'odd' or nervous in front of them and sometimes avoids eye contact. After social situations are over, she replays the conversations in her head and ruminates over the things she said and how she believes she came across. She then typically feels depressed and dreads seeing her friends again. This sometimes leads her to cancel or drop out of social events at the last minute, and her friends start to leave her out of planned events, which only proves in Romy's mind that her friends do think she is boring.

Illustrative example

Hussein suffers from panic attacks. These attacks have typically occurred in crowded places, such as on public transport and in shopping areas. Hussain believes that he will be unable to breathe and will collapse in public, so he avoids using any form of transport and walks miles to work. When walking, he ensures he does not elevate his heart too much and takes frequent breaks to 'catch his breath'. He also avoids any activity that he thinks will elevate his heart rate, such as playing sports. Hussein will also not go into a shop by himself in case he collapses and needs help to get home. When he cannot avoid going out on his own, he uses nasal sprays to help him breathe and stays near benches and rails so he has something to hold on to if he does collapse.

Mood-based behaviour

According to the *DSM-5* diagnostic classification system (APA, 2013), depressive disorders (classified as mood disorders in the previous edition, *DSM-IV-TR* (APA, 2004)) are a group of diagnoses where the common feature is the presence of sadness, irritability or empty mood. Mood-based behaviour refers to the tendency for an individual to act in accordance with a prevailing mood state. Behaviours borne out of depressed mood states, such as social withdrawal, reduced activity and AVOIDANCE, increase feelings of helplessness and hopelessness.

> **Illustrative example**
>
> Gary has been depressed for many months. Most days his mood is very low and everyday tasks seem insurmountable. He takes little pleasure in doing the things that used to lift his mood, such as walking the dog. On the days when he doesn't walk the dog, he feels intensely guilty and turns to wine to numb his mood, making it harder to get up the next day. He berates himself for not being able to put as much effort into his work as he used to and believes he has no reason to be depressed. He feels ashamed about seeking psychological support. He believes his partner deserves better but feels unable to make the effort to be upbeat around him. He avoids seeing his friends as he thinks he will only bring them down. He spends most weekends in bed, doesn't attend to household tasks and often avoids responding to important work emails.

Gary's example shows how disorders such as depression are worsened and perpetuated by mood-based behaviour. Unwittingly, Gary is doing exactly what his depressed mood dictates, thereby feeding his depression. Scheduling small, manageable tasks into a depressed client's day is often a first step in the treatment of depression. But before trying to help the client get better, the CBT therapist needs to stop the client from making themselves worse. This is not to imply that the client is to blame for their low mood; it is very difficult to act against overwhelming negative feelings.

Strategies to avoid negative affect

When a client holds rigid rules and beliefs, they are vulnerable to intensely uncomfortable feelings when those rules are broken. Therefore, the client may develop behavioural strategies to avoid activating AVERSIVE EMOTIONS. Unfortunately, such strategies reinforce unhelpful ways of thinking.

> **Illustrative example**
> Debbie believes that if she 'lets down' her friends in any way, then she is a terrible person. She never says 'no' to requests from friends because, if she did, she would feel intense guilt. As a result, Debbie often fails to act in her own best interests and frequently ends up doing things she doesn't want to do (or hasn't time to do) for the benefit of others. When her friends do not reciprocate the efforts she puts into maintaining friendships, she often feels hurt and angry, but she does not tell her friends of these feelings.

Because Debbie understandably wishes to avoid discomfort associated with feelings of intense guilt, she lets herself be pushed around. Instead of learning to bear her discomfort and challenge her belief that she must not let others down, her overly compliant behaviour reinforces this unhealthy attitude. In CBT treatment, Debbie would be encouraged to desist from behaviour designed to stave off aversive guilt feelings and modify her beliefs that produce disproportionate guilt in the first place. She would also be encouraged to update her belief about such specific reciprocity in friendships and allow her friends to not always make the same effort she chooses to make, and to communicate her feelings of hurt or anger appropriately, so her friends can change their behaviour, should they wish to.

This is just one example of an emotional state that individuals will make self-defeating efforts to avoid. There are many others, such as shame, ANXIETY, jealousy and so on.

Goal-setting and homework

From the very first session, CBT treatment involves identifying specific emotional and practical problems that the client is grappling with. A problem list is developed and, from this list, specific goals for therapy are developed. Goals in CBT are carefully negotiated between the therapist and client to ensure that they are specific, measurable, achievable, realistic and time-bound. These are represented by the acronym 'SMART'.

S: *Specific.* Goals pertain to specific examples of target problems. It is not enough, for example, to accept a goal of 'feeling less anxious'. Where and when the client wishes to feel less ANXIETY needs to be precisely defined – i.e. 'To be able to go shopping in my local grocery store without feeling anxious.'

M: *Measurable.* There needs to be a mechanism for monitoring progress toward the specific goal. Sometimes psychometric measures can be used for this purpose. The Beck Depression Inventory (BDI) is commonly used to monitor severity of depression. Subjective Units of Distress Scales (SUDS) can be useful when monitoring goal progression in ANXIETY disorders. The client may also be encouraged to keep a log of their progress, where they can record even small positive changes that may otherwise be overlooked or quickly forgotten.

A: *Achievable.* Goals need to be within the client's scope to achieve. Essentially, goals need to be tailored to meet the client's existing skill set. Any skill deficits need to be addressed, and rectified where appropriate. For example, a client may need some assertiveness training. Goals also need to be dependent on the effort of the client themself. Goals that include changing other people's behaviour are not useful, because other people are not within the client's sphere of control. So, a goal 'To stop other people from making unreasonable demands on me' is not acceptable, whereas the goal 'To be able to assert myself in the face of unreasonable demands from others' is achievable.

R: *Realistic.* There is little point in accepting a therapeutic goal that the client is unlikely to be able to achieve. To do so only sets the client up to fail. It is important to take into account the place the client is starting from when agreeing goals. Hence, if a client's extreme social ANXIETY leads them to avoid talking in social groups, it is not realistic to agree a goal of becoming a stand-up comic. A more realistic goal would be 'to be able to talk freely in small social groups'.

T: *Time bound.* Some goals will be short term and others medium or long term. It is not always possible to accurately estimate how long it will take an individual to realise their specific goals. It is prudent, however, to place goals within some sort of time frame. Doing so lends structure to the treatment and promotes consistent client effort. CBT therapists need to exercise caution when setting time frames. Too long a period may discourage the client or lead to complacency. Too short a time frame may overwhelm the client or lead them to further feelings of hopelessness if they fail to meet the deadline. Ideally, time frames for goal achievement will be kept quite flexible so a balance can be struck between keeping the client motivated and guarding against possible self-recrimination.

The principle of INTERACTIONALISM and mutual reinforcement dictates that goals ideally ought to include both an emotional and functional component.

Using the fictional examples of Romy, Hussein, Gary and Debbie outlined above, typical problems and goals may be composed thus:

Problem: Romy suffers with social ANXIETY and will not assert her opinion spontaneously with friends.
Goal: To be able to assert an opinion in front of friends without structuring it in advance and with significantly less ANXIETY.

Problem: Hussein suffers panic attacks in public places.
Goal: To be able to go on public transport and into shopping areas while feeling nervous but not panicky.

Problem: Gary is depressed and has greatly reduced functioning.
Goal: To keep to an activity schedule and alleviate feelings of depression.

Problem: Debbie is unassertive and experiences severe guilt if she 'lets friends down'.
Goal: For Debbie to be able to say 'no' to friends' requests without feeling intense guilt.

Note that the hypothetical problems and goals listed above include both an affective and a behavioural component. Goals stated with this dual emphasis afford the opportunity to work simultaneously on COGNITIVE RESTRUCTURING and behavioural modification. The client is encouraged to re-jig their thinking against a pre-existing negative belief and in support of a healthier alternative, as in Hussein's case: 'I can't cope with ANXIETY-provoking situations' versus 'I can cope in ANXIETY-provoking situations despite uncomfortable feelings.' They are also encouraged to experience the truth of new beliefs through action. To continue with the example of Hussein, he practises holding his new coping belief while going on the Underground, thereby learning that, although the journey was not pleasant, he did, in fact, survive it without calamity. Hussein's belief in his ability to cope with unpleasant feelings and difficult situations is enhanced and his notion that danger is imminent is eroded. Through the repetition of such 'exposure'-based exercises, belief change is deepened and anchored. This process is often referred to in CBT literature and basic psychological parlance as HABITUATION.

In light of the above, homework assignments will be collaboratively devised and agreed between therapist and client. The homework will follow logically from the session work and will promote goal attainment. As with goal-setting, homework needs to be devised carefully. Dryden and Branch (2008) discuss the principle of setting 'challenging but not overwhelming' between-session assignments. So, homework will ideally be sufficiently challenging to propel the client outside of their comfort zone but also be within range of what they are currently able to achieve. It is common for CBT therapists to build a graded hierarchy with their clients. This involves identifying goal-related tasks and ranking them in order of perceived difficulty. The idea is to move up the hierarchy from the lowest-ranking items to the highest. The speed at which the client moves up the hierarchy will depend on several factors, such as:

- client willingness to experience short-term discomfort in order to achieve long-term gain
- severity and duration of the client's presenting problem
- the quality of the therapeutic relationship
- the therapist ensuring that the client adequately understands the rationale behind behavioural work
- other emotional/psychological problems that may become evident through behavioural work and require therapeutic attention (for example, shame is a common emotional obstacle to therapeutic progress)
- environmental factors.

The skilled CBT therapist will bear these factors in mind throughout treatment and be sensitive to their potential interference.

Another important point to bear in mind with regard to behavioural interventions is that the client will be expected to carry out tasks that will, almost inevitably, cause them a degree of emotional discomfort. While the ultimate goal may be to eliminate ANXIETY, guilt or depression, the road to this goal will be paved with effort and, regrettably, pain. So, although it would be highly desirable that Gary goes through the allotted tasks on his activity schedule without any discomfort, this is very unlikely to be the case. Instead, he may have to be encouraged to grit his teeth and drag himself from one task to the next, despite his profound feelings of lethargy and hopelessness. Eventually, it will become easier, but it can take some time. Hussein, too, will be asked to agree to go into ANXIETY-provoking situations while feeling anxious and still learning to bear those intensely uncomfortable feelings. Again, eventually, his belief in his ability to cope with anxious feelings will increase and his fear of certain circumstances will begin to diminish. Debbie will be encouraged to decline requests from friends but also to expect to feel very uncomfortable about it for some time, until she gets used to saying 'no'. It takes time for COGNITIVE and behavioural change to result in emotional change. Emotion is rather like the last coach on the train.

The setting and reviewing of homework will frequently constitute the bulk of the middle phase of CBT treatment. The therapeutic benefits of between-session homework are many:

- Therapeutic learning is transported outside of the consulting room and into the client's daily life.
- Therapy time is maximised through the use of between-session practice.
- Client independence and ownership of the therapy is promoted.
- The client adopts valuable coping strategies.
- Therapy moves from the philosophical and cerebral towards the practical.
- Much is to be learnt by both client and therapist through homework assignments, be they 'successful' or 'unsuccessful'. (If the client fails to complete homework or execute it as outlined, then obstacles can be identified and dealt with accordingly.)
- Thoughtful homework construction and review between

therapist and client may indicate to the client that their therapist is truly interested in their recovery, and this may strengthen the alliance.

The work CBT therapists expect their clients to carry out is neither easy nor painless. Thus, the CBT practitioner needs to be empathic, and to compassionately 'cajole' the client along. The client's successes and efforts ought never to go unnoticed by the CBT therapist. To this end, many CBT therapists encourage their clients to keep a positive data record in which they write down their efforts and the therapeutic rewards of their hard work. CBT trainees are sometimes invited to consider what they would be prepared to do in order to overcome their own difficulties. Would you ask a client to do something that you, as a therapist, would not be prepared to do yourself?

Behavioural activation

As with CBT, behavioural activation (BA) theory is rooted in the work of behaviourist B.F. Skinner. In the 1970s, behaviourists such as Ferster (Skinner & Ferster, 1970) and Lewinsohn furthered the behavioural movement towards a behavioural treatment for depression. Lewinsohn (1974) proposed that, when people lose major sources of positive reinforcement, they are vulnerable to depression. BA aims to activate clients in specific ways that increase rewarding experiences. BA therefore focuses on processes that inhibit activation, such as AVOIDANCE.

Whereas CBT targets both COGNITION and behaviour throughout treatment to change how people feel, BA foregrounds behavioural change as a first-line intervention to help change how people feel. BA suggests that life stressors can lead to depression and the short-term coping strategies that people use may actually be keeping them stuck. Clients are given specific, structured behavioural activities that they are encouraged to follow, regardless of mood, and emphasis is placed on activities that are naturally reinforcing.

As discussed in Chapter 2, CBT makes use of the ABC MODEL, and highlights its INTERACTIONAL nature. BA, conversely, proposes a 'functional analysis' (see Figure 7.1): that when an antecedent (A) occurs, a behaviour (B) will occur, and the consequences (C) of the behaviour dictate whether it increases or decreases.

Figure 7.1: Functional analysis (Martell et al., 2010)

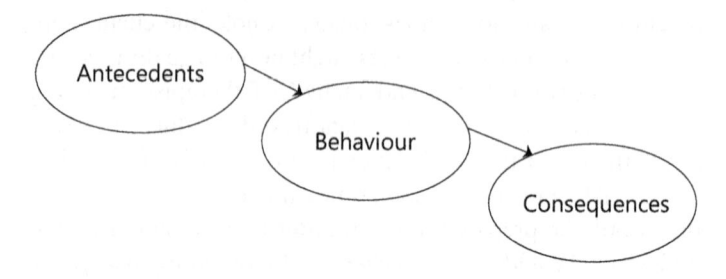

Antecedents → Behaviour → Consequences

In 1996 Jacobson and colleagues proposed that CT for depression (Beck et al., 1979) could be split into three components:

1. activity scheduling
2. COGNITIVE RESTRUCTURING that includes activity scheduling
3. CT treatment that includes activity scheduling, COGNITIVE RESTRUCTURING and CORE BELIEF work.

They found that there was no evidence to support the hypothesis that a 'full package' of CT has better results than the other components. Moreover, CT was no more effective than BA (activity scheduling) in preventing relapse two years post-treatment (Kanter et al., 2009). This served to further reignite research into BA for the treatment of depression.

In 2003, Hopko and colleagues compared BA with an alternative version of BA known as brief behavioural activation treatment for depression (BATD). Both BA and BATD attempt to make sense of a client's behaviour in terms of its functionality, and therefore schedule activities based on function. A noticeable difference between BA and BATD is that the latter also incorporates how other people may be able to support the client in becoming behaviourally activated (Hopko et al., 2003). BA and BATD make much use of homework, and homework tasks are reviewed at the subsequent session. Types of homework will broadly include activity and mood monitoring, activity scheduling, activity structuring (or grades tasks similar to those used in Beck's CT for depression), prevention of rumination (attention to experiences exercises) and maintaining an activation focus (Martell et al., 2010).

BA is currently recommended by the National Institute for Health and Care Excellence (NICE, 2009) as an evidenced-based treatment for adults with severe depression, and research into its efficacy into different populations is ongoing (see Tindall et al., 2017 for a review of BA as a treatment for depression in young people).

A detailed discussion of BA is beyond the scope of this book, but there is some suggested further reading in Appendix 1.

Chapter 8
Methods of discovering assumptions, rules and core beliefs

Examination of assumptions, rules and CORE BELIEFS will normally take place after the client has become very familiar with the CBT model and is beginning to apply it to specific everyday problems. Ideally, the client will have completed homework assignments aimed at spotting and challenging their NEGATIVE AUTOMATIC THOUGHTS (NATS), with some degree of success. Catching and arresting NATS serves to shake the foundations of underlying belief systems and may potentially render CORE BELIEFS more accessible to the client. Having done homework on NATS also helps to ensure that the client has sufficient confidence in the model and their skills in applying it before unearthing more fundamentally held beliefs. If this is not the case and deeper belief work begins hastily, the client may feel overwhelmed or endangered and react defensively. It is incumbent on the CBT therapist to be sensitive to the client's state of readiness before beginning this and all stages of CBT.

The therapeutic importance of being prudent about timing is made clear by Neenan and Dryden (2004, p.161):

> To tackle these beliefs before this stage has been reached may result in clients feeling overwhelmed, threatened, distressed or resistant and lead to premature termination of therapy.

Assessing assumptions and rules

Once the CBT therapist has satisfied themselves that the client is ready to start working on assumptions and rules, one or more of the following strategies can be used.

If–then statements

Dysfunctional assumptions are frequently expressed in causal 'if x occurs then y follows' language. Assumptions can also be articulated as conditional statements, such as, 'Unless I accomplish x then y will surely follow.' The initial 'if' or 'unless' component of the assertion dictates what the client believes they must either achieve or avoid. The secondary 'then' component outlines the negative event that the client believes will ensue should they fail to do so. For example:

- Unless I always please my partner, then they will leave me for someone else.
- If I do not take on all work assignments asked of me, then my boss will fire me.
- Unless I am always entertaining and fun, then my friends will stop liking me.
- If I let others know I suffer with ANXIETY, then they will lose all respect for me.

Perhaps the most commonly used method of eliciting faulty assumptions via an 'if/unless–then' statement is to provide the client with the 'if' component and allow them to fill in the blanks.

Illustrative example

Stevie is a dedicated teacher at a primary school. She gets on well with her colleagues and sometimes spends time with them outside of work. There is a clear atmosphere of stress in the school and many teachers complain about the workload and discuss openly how overwhelmed they feel. They often ask each other to share lesson plans, which Stevie happily does. However, despite being overwhelmed

> herself, she chooses not to vocalise this with the other teachers. She often spends her weekends working on her lesson plans for the following week and works late in the evenings researching new ones.

Therapist: Okay, Stevie, so you'd like to be able to ask for help when you need it at work. It sounds like that would help you to control your stress levels more effectively. Have you recently avoided asking for help at work?

Stevie: Last week I had to plan a lesson I hadn't taught before and I really would have benefitted from seeing a few lesson-plan ideas. But I just couldn't bring myself to ask the other teachers.

Therapist: I see. Would it be helpful for us to work out why you couldn't bring yourself to ask to see the other teachers for their lesson plans?

Stevie: Yes, I think so.

Therapist: Okay. I'm going to provide you with the first half of a sentence and I'd like you to complete it for me: If I ask for help with the lesson plan…

Stevie: … then the other teachers will know I can't come up with a good idea. They'll think I can't do it without their help.

Therapist: And if they think you need their help…

Stevie: … then they may think I'm not going to make it as a teacher; I'd feel incompetent.

Therapist: What do you think about the endings you gave to those sentences I started? Any clues there about why you might be finding it so difficult to ask for help from teachers at work?

Stevie: I think that I must be able to do everything at work without help or it means I'm incompetent.

At this point, the CBT therapist will record the last statement Stevie made and begin helping her to test out whether or not this assumption is wholly true and helpful.

It is worth mentioning that Stevie's judgement of herself as 'incompetent' in the work domain may indicate an all-pervasive CORE BELIEF of incompetence. At this stage, this is merely a hunch, however. The CBT therapist may make a mental note of this for later investigation, if it seems appropriate.

Recognising themes

Another way of teasing out personal rules and assumptions is to look for recurrent themes in the client's automatic thoughts. Client and therapist review together daily thought records (DTRs) and ABC forms (see Chapter 6) that the client has completed in several different situations. Frequently, we find that the client is expressing the same sentiment in various different forms. Here are some examples of Stevie's automatic thoughts that she recorded in her DTR:

Situation: Not being able to sync her email on her phone.

Thought: I should've been able to work that out myself.

Situation: Not being able to get the smart board at work to show a picture.

Thought: I've used this board before so I should be able to make it work.

Situation: Getting lost while driving to a friend's house.

Thought: Everyone else got there fine, I'm an idiot for getting lost.

Situation: Hosting a dinner party.

Thought: I've got to make sure that everyone has a nice time.

Stevie's therapist spotted a theme in her automatic thinking: namely, that Stevie takes responsibility for doing things by herself without any external assistance. The therapist then put this to Stevie, thereby inviting her to extract the underlying rule for living embodied in her NATS:

Therapist: Looking at this DTR, you seem to habitually expect yourself to be able to sort things out. Do you agree with that, Stevie?

Stevie: Yeah, I suppose so, but I feel like, because it's possible to do those things without help, I should be able to do them without help.

Therapist: And if you aren't able to do whatever needs doing by yourself...?

Stevie: I just won't accept it. It would mean I'm not putting in enough effort.

Therapist: And if you're not putting in enough effort, what would you conclude that meant about you?

Stevie: That I'm not working hard enough, which would mean I'm lazy or, worse still, I am putting in the effort but I'm just incompetent.

After this brief exchange, it becomes clear that Stevie's MALADAPTIVE ASSUMPTION is, 'If I can't do everything by myself then I am incompetent.'

Highlighting imperative statements

Rules and assumptions often include imperatives such as 'should', 'must', 'ought to', 'need to', 'have to' and 'got to'. These imperatives are rigid and non-negotiable, leaving no room for deviation or error. We can see some of these clearly represented in Stevie's automatic thoughts in the preceding section. When a client starts articulating imperative statements about herself and her behaviour, it is generally a reliable signpost to a strongly held rule for living. Almost invariably, there will be a perceived negative consequence or punishment attached to breaking a 'should/must'-based personal rule. Often this will be an affective consequence, such as guilt, shame or depression. The client may sometimes be more readily able to identify a negative self-evaluative consequence, such as 'I'm incompetent', than an affective one. It is a circular argument, however, since a negative self-appraisal leads to a negative emotional response, and vice versa.

Urging clients to notice their 'should' statements is another way of helping them to identify unhealthy assumptions. In the following example transcript, Stevie first gives an emotional consequence for breaking her rules. The therapist uses this information to ask further questions that reveal Stevie's negative self-evaluation.

Therapist: Stevie, you've stated on a few occasions that you should or must be able to do things, like figure out your email, how to use the smart screen at work, or be able to get to places without getting lost. Would you agree that you use that type of 'no other option' language quite frequently with yourself?

Stevie: Yeah, now you point it out, I think I do.

Therapist: So, what do you imagine would be the result if you weren't able to do something you strongly believed you should be able to do? For example, if we look at how you viewed getting lost while driving to your friend's house.

Stevie: Well, I was stupid. I had driven there before. I was ashamed of myself, I guess.

Therapist: And what is so shame-provoking about getting lost?

Stevie: I should have been able to find my way.

Therapist: So, if I can clarify, to your way of thinking, you should have been able to find your way and because you couldn't you are...

Stevie: Stupid and incompetent.

After this exchange, Stevie's assumption becomes clear. It is also becoming more evident that Stevie readily resorts to labelling herself 'incompetent' or 'stupid' both in the work domain and outside of it. This lends greater credence to the hunch that this may be a CORE BELIEF.

Charting highs and lows in mood

Because dysfunctional assumptions or rules are typically unyielding and extreme, they tend to produce extreme (often disproportionate) emotional responses in clients, when they are either met or unmet. It is often very useful not only to pay attention to the client's low mood but also to investigate what lies

84   *The Cognitive Behaviour Therapy Primer*

behind a 'high' mood. When a client is able to fulfil an assumption or live up to a personal rule, they may experience profound relief and even temporary euphoria. Simply because the client is feeling good doesn't mean that it is not for problematic reasons. Using the type of questioning represented in the fictional transcript below can be a very efficient method of getting to the bottom of a client's underlying belief system. We will return to the example of Stevie, for the sake of consistency and clarity.

Therapist: So the dinner party went well, Stevie?

Stevie: Yeah, really well. I had loads of comments about the food, which fortunately turned out really well. Everyone seemed to like it and they said they'd want to come again.

Therapist: Great. So how do you feel about the dinner turning out so well?

Stevie: Awesome, it was a massive mood lift. I really needed an ego boost, so that was great.

Therapist: Well, I'm glad that you're feeling so good at the moment. But, at the risk of putting a bit of a dampener on things, can I ask you another question? I'll explain my reasons in a moment.

Stevie: Well, sure, I guess. Go ahead.

Therapist: Thank you. How do you imagine you'd be feeling if the dinner hadn't been so well received by your friends?

Stevie: You mean, if they didn't like the food?

Therapist: Well, either it wasn't well received at all or even if it was just a bit mediocre?

Stevie: Umm...

Therapist: Think about it for a minute. Try to imagine it going less well. How do you think you'd be feeling right now?

Stevie: Well, I'd feel crap. I definitely wouldn't want to do it again. Probably wouldn't want to talk about it with them. I don't think I could face it.

Therapist: That sounds like a pretty intense response to throwing a mediocre dinner party. What do you think?

Stevie: I'd certainly feel really embarrassed and depressed about it, yeah. The thought of having them round again would make me really anxious.

Therapist: So, while it is good that it did go well, the important point to note is that, because you so strongly believe that you have to throw an excellent dinner party, you'd feel profoundly distressed if you failed to do so.

Stevie: Yeah, that's true.

Therapist: And because you met your rule about throwing an excellent dinner party, you feel profoundly good about having done so.

Stevie: That's true too. So, are you saying I shouldn't be as happy about it as I am?

Therapist: Not exactly. I'm trying to highlight to you the assumption that I think you hold – namely, 'If I throw an excellent dinner party, then I'm an okay person.' Do you agree that you hold that type of assumption?

Stevie: Yeah, I must do. So, what does that mean about how good I felt about it then?

Therapist: Only that, as your therapist, I'd like to encourage you to feel great about the dinner party going well but also understand that you would still be an okay person even if it had been mediocre or, indeed, flopped. Does that make sense?

Stevie: Yeah, I need to be more okay with it not going well but can feel good when it does go well.

From this point the therapist would continue to discuss with Stevie how currently her self-worth is contingent on her underlying assumptions/rules being met. Stevie would then be encouraged to consider how modifying her rules would enable her to be more flexible and to adapt to negative events, like throwing an average dinner party, while still being able to think well of herself as a person. Stevie might be encouraged to chart her moods and search for the assumptions underlying any extreme variations.

Exposing core beliefs

CORE BELIEFS can be conceptualised as being a layer beneath assumptions and rules, which are basically on the same level and used interchangeably. After NATS and assumptions have been elicited and restructured, CORE BELIEFS are the next target area. In contrast to assumptions, CORE BELIEFS tend to be stated as definitive facts. As discussed in Chapter 3, they pertain to idiosyncratic beliefs the client holds to be unquestionably true about themselves, other people and the world. As such, they are notoriously difficult therapeutic territory to navigate.

Examples of three typical CORE BELIEFS are:

Self: I am weak.
Others: People are ruthless.
World/life: Life is stacked against me.

Not every client will desire to or benefit from working at the CORE BELIEF level. Some clients will be content to leave therapy after they have managed to change a few dysfunctional assumptions and are benefitting from the associated symptom relief. In order to work effectively at the CORE BELIEF level, treatment will need to be long term (perhaps a year or more, in some cases) and client consent is essential. Under no circumstances should the therapist insist that the client remain in treatment post-improvement if the client does not wish to do so. First, duration of treatment is essentially up to the client, and second, any form of coercion flies in the face of the principle of collaboration that underpins CBT practice.

However, if a client wishes to work at a deeper level of COGNITION, then there are various methods of pinpointing CORE BELIEFS available to the CBT therapist.

The downward arrow

This method is also used to identify assumptions and rules. It involves eliciting AFFECT-LADEN thoughts, temporarily assuming that these thoughts are true and then further eliciting the meaning assigned to them until a baseline belief is revealed. The baseline BELIEF arrived at following this process is likely to be CORE. Unlike when working at the level of NEGATIVE AUTOMATIC THOUGHTS, with the downward arrow technique, thoughts are neither challenged nor answered back; if they were, it would arrest the downward progression of the arrow. The therapist asks brief, meaning-focused questions designed to move the client further into the core of the therapist's thinking. Even if the therapist has hunches about the client's CORE BELIEFS based on earlier NATS and assumption work, they will keep these to themself during the downward arrow exercise. It is important that the client is given ample time to focus on the questions asked and that their answers are generated entirely from their own introspection.

In order to use this method effectively, it helps to adhere to the following points:

1. Identify a specific situation or typical example of the target problem.
2. If the client has specified a negative emotional state, use this to drive your questioning in the first instance.
3. Use leading questions, such as 'What then?' and 'If that were true, what would that mean?', to elicit further conclusions from the client.
4. When you seem to have arrived at an endgame, complete your questioning with 'And what would you decide that meant about you?' or 'And what do you conclude about yourself, in that case?' The client's response to this question will very likely be a CORE BELIEF about themself.

The sample transcript below shows how her therapist used the downward arrow technique to find Stevie's CORE BELIEF about herself that was triggering her ANXIETY about being observed by an Ofsted inspector.

Therapist: So, Stevie, what specifically do you find ANXIETY-provoking about being observed by the Ofsted inspector?

Stevie: Well, it's an important observation that affects the school rating and is shared with the headteacher.

Therapist: And what is ANXIETY-provoking about it affecting the school rating and being known to the head teacher?

Stevie: That I might not get a good rating; that I perform poorly.

Therapist: And if you did perform poorly, what would that mean?

Stevie: The teachers and the head would know I did a bad job.

Therapist: And if others knew you didn't perform well?

Stevie: That they think I'm crap, that I am a rubbish teacher.

Therapist: And if they did think that you are a rubbish teacher, what would you conclude about yourself?

Stevie: I'd agree, it would mean I am a rubbish teacher.

Therapist: Would it stop at rubbish teacher, or would you also decide it meant something about you as a person?

Stevie: That I was incompetent as a person.

In this case, the downward arrow revealed a CORE BELIEF Stevie holds about herself: 'I'm rubbish/incompetent.' The same technique can be used to discover CORE BELIEFS about others and the world.

Review of relevant historical experiences

The CORE BELIEFS we hold today usually have tendrils reaching into the past. CORE BELIEFS are generally formed in early life as a result of myriad factors, including family learning, traumas, particularly salient experiences, societal influences, cultural and religious norms and influences from peers or other significant adults. Sometimes we fail to update our early belief systems; our ideas about ourselves, others and the world remain frozen, despite subsequent adult experiences and learning that may contradict their validity. CBT therapists will often ask clients when they think a particular assumption or CORE BELIEF first occurred to them. Often the client will be able to recite an incident or series of incidents that led them to form specific conclusions about themselves and the world around them. This can be therapeutically invaluable, as the client is then able to revisit these early experiences and assign more accurate and helpful meanings to them, thus updating their dysfunctional CORE BELIEFS and assumptions (see Chapter 6).

When the client and therapist are still on a quest to unearth CORE BELIEFS, questions about the past can be equally useful. When Stevie's therapist asked her about childhood and early life events that may have contributed toward her assumption that she must do everything on her own or view herself as incompetent, this is what she found out.

Stevie was one of four children. Her parents separated when she was seven and, although the divorce was amicable, both parents struggled financially. Succeeding at school was strongly encouraged by both parents, and education was highly valued. There was an explicit message given to all the children that they should work hard so as not to have to struggle financially in the way their parents did. Stevie remembers the family always being short of money, and her father would often stress how important it was to him that she should be able to fend for herself. She remembers the family not having as much money as her friends' families.

This belief also extended beyond money, to self-reliance. There were several occasions when Stevie asked for help with her homework and her dad would encourage her to persevere and try to figure it out herself. On one occasion, Stevie forgot to take an important item to school and rushed home in tears, begging her mum to help her find it so she could return with it before school started. Stevie remembers telling her mother how worried she was and how awful she thought going to school without it would be. She desperately wanted her mother to calm her down and help her find it. She recalls her mother saying, 'Worse things than this will happen to you, you should have been more organised.'

From these hypothetical early experiences, it is fairly easy to see how Stevie developed the belief that she must do things under her own steam and that, should she fail to do so, then it meant she was intrinsically incompetent. Despite the fact that Stevie's parents were probably acting in accordance with what they believed was best for Stevie in the long run, she developed some very hindering ideas about herself.

This made-up example illustrates that any type of early experience can ultimately lead to the formation of both ADAPTIVE and MALADAPTIVE beliefs. Care received from parental figures need not be deliberately abusive or malicious or blatantly nurturing or benevolent to contribute to CORE BELIEF formation. Similarly, while extreme or unusual events do tend to significantly inform an individual's understanding of the world, mundane events repeated over time can also carry profound influential weight.

Delving into meaning

The idiosyncratic meanings clients give to their experiences can be exposed effectively through the downward arrow technique. Another very simple method of pinpointing CORE BELIEFS involves getting the client to fill in the blanks:

I am...
Other people are...
The world is...

Sometimes CORE BELIEFS are fully articulated in the form of NATS. Reviewing NATS may bring to light probable CORE BELIEFS such as, 'I'm so useless', 'Nobody likes me', 'People are out to get me' and so on. If these types of NATS are consistently recorded, it can be useful to investigate how deeply the client believes them in order to determine if they are core.

These shortcuts can sometimes work very well. However, it is advisable to use them either in conjunction with one of the other methods discussed above or as a last resort when other methods have been unsuccessful.

To summarise

The meanings assigned to events from the past theoretically result in CORE BELIEFS, as we have seen in the example of Stevie. Current, anticipated and recent events then reactivate these CORE BELIEFS. In essence, TRIGGER EVENTS activate NATS and assumptions, which confirm and reinforce the apparent validity of negative CORE BELIEFS. Therefore COGNITION (beliefs, rules, assumptions) critically influences, and potentially skews, interpretation of events. This illustrates the powerful interactive relationship between event interpretation, COGNITION, emotion and behaviour.

Chapter 9
Relapse prevention and endings

In this chapter we will discuss CBT's somewhat unique position on maintaining and safeguarding therapeutic gains through collaborative planning and troubleshooting. We will also look at how endings are structured and negotiated in CBT.

Planning for and preventing relapse

Relapse prevention is an important part of the final phase of CBT treatment. In the spirit of helping the client to become their own therapist, therapeutic gains are revisited and consolidated during the middle and final stages of treatment. Psychological improvement is attributed to the client's hard work and perseverance. This is not only an accurate representation of how improvement has been achieved; it also bolsters the client's confidence in their ability to maintain their psychological wellbeing after regular CBT sessions have ended.

Generally, CBT therapists will discuss openly with their clients the possibility of symptom resurgence or relapse. While there is no harm (and certainly there may be benefit) in taking an optimistic stance toward the client's continued improvement, clinical experience suggests that some degree of relapse is likely in most cases. It is therefore important to prepare clients for possible setbacks *en route* to wholesome recovery. This preparation normalises relapse and helps the client to view setbacks as a common part of recovery, rather than a return to square one. By endorsing this viewpoint, the client can effectively predispose themself to feel disappointed but not utterly devastated in the event of relapse. The return of symptoms is distressing enough without the added fear that all that has been gained through treatment is now lost. Through thoughtful collaborative planning for the possibility of relapse, the client is more likely to view setbacks as an opportunity for valuable review and practice. Setbacks can also provide opportunities for further learning.

The term 'relapse prevention' is something of a misnomer. The name suggests that this stage of CBT therapy is aimed at simply preventing problems from returning. From what has been discussed above, it becomes clear that there is more to relapse prevention planning than the term suggests. The aim is not only to prevent relapse but also to prepare the client to manage and overcome it, should it occur.

For clients with enduring or chronic problems such as OBSESSIVE-COMPULSIVE DISORDER (OCD), addiction, chronic pain or treatment-resistant depression, relapse prevention is paramount. In these cases, relapse is unfortunately more likely to be the norm than the exception. Clients with chronic conditions are often helped to view managing their symptoms as a lifelong endeavour. Lifestyle changes, behavioural exercises and managing intrusive thoughts are some of the more important aspects of recovery for this client group. Continued regular practice is frequently found to be essential and is a predictor of sustained improvement. Maintaining positive change and being alert to early warning signs of problems returning are key aspects of relapse prevention planning for every client, but of particular relevance to clients with chronic conditions.

The main points pertaining to relapse prevention (to be considered with the client) are divided into categories and outlined below. A relapse prevention worksheet is included at Appendix 2 and provides a summary of the main points discussed here. This can be adapted to fit each client and completed with the client towards the end of therapy. Clients then have a summary of the key therapeutic interventions that were helpful and can refer to it post-treatment should they need to. There are also several ready-made relapse prevention forms that the CBT therapist may choose to use. Literature that pertains to CBT treatment for a specific disorder (i.e. PTSD) often have a relapse prevention plan that pertains to relevant therapy areas covered during treatment for that disorder.

Reviewing problems and goals

When striving to consolidate therapeutic learning and change, it pays to revisit the original problem/s and associated goal/s. This reminds both client and therapist how much progress has been made since treatment first began. Such a review also highlights what the client needs to pay attention to when planning to prevent and surmount relapse. We strongly recommend being very precise when responding to the relapse prevention-related questions posed in this section and the sections that follow.

Throughout CBT treatment, it is expected that the therapist will be highly specific. Specificity clarifies and solidifies points in an individual's mind; the client is more likely to retain concise specific points than vague concepts.

The following questions can be useful for client and therapist to answer together:

- What were the original presenting problems that brought the client to treatment? These can be separated into emotional, behavioural, interpersonal and environmental or practical problem categories. Psychiatric diagnosis can also be noted, if applicable.
- What goals were set in relation to these problems? Goals can also be clearly outlined by separating them into the same categories: emotional, behavioural, interpersonal and environmental or practical.
- What goal-directed change has been made thus far? Specificity is key.
- What are the benefits of therapeutic change/progress made thus far? The pay-offs of hard work and effort can

be surprisingly easily forgotten and taken for granted. Reviewing the benefits of goal-directed activity can help to renew client motivation. Here again it is good practice to be highly specific about the areas where benefits have been experienced.

Reviewing belief change

Although not every client will have worked on modifying MALADAPTIVE CORE BELIEFS, most will have achieved some COGNITIVE RESTRUCTURING with regard to assumptions by the time therapy is terminated. Certainly most clients will have identified their thinking errors and NEGATIVE AUTOMATIC THOUGHTS (NATS). Even clients who have experienced primarily behavioural interventions (as in the case of panic disorder, for example) and less overt COGNITIVE RESTRUCTURING will have changed important attitudes. Most CBT therapists will have one eye on attitude and belief change when considering relapse prevention. Recapping on and reinforcing positive belief and attitudinal change is therefore a crucial aspect of relapse prevention planning. The following is a guideline for charting belief change:

- What negative CORE BELIEFS have been identified (if applicable)?
    - Self:
    - Others:
    - World:
- What healthy alternative CORE BELIEFS have been established and strengthened through treatment (if applicable)?
    - Self:
    - Others:
    - World:
- What MALADAPTIVE ASSUMPTIONS and rules have been identified?
- What ADAPTIVE ALTERNATIVE ASSUMPTIONS have been developed?

- What thinking errors does the client typically make?
- What realistic interpretations has the client devised to counteract their thinking errors?
- What skills has the client acquired for 'answering back to' or challenging their NATs?

Recognising triggers

TRIGGERS are events or circumstances that activate negative CORE BELIEFS and attitudes. As such, TRIGGER EVENTS tend to give rise to psychological distress or disturbance. The same TRIGGERS that sparked off a client's original problems are worth revisiting when constructing a relapse prevention plan. Through the course of treatment, clients may develop 'immunity' to particular TRIGGERS that once caused them difficulty. Yet it is still worth acknowledging past TRIGGERS as potential problem areas in the future. It is also worth 'upping the ante' by encouraging the client to imagine different or more extreme scenarios that may be likely to trigger unhealthy beliefs, emotions and behaviours. This gives the client the chance to fortify their therapeutic defences against relapse, should such events actually occur. The following is a guideline for reviewing past TRIGGERS and highlighting potential ones:

- What types of situations or conditions have typically triggered unhealthy CORE BELIEFS/MALADAPTIVE ASSUMPTIONS/NATs or thinking errors?
    - past environmental TRIGGERS (i.e. illness, financial worry, work hassles, seasonal changes, household bills, moving house and so forth)
    - past interpersonal TRIGGERS (i.e. relationship conflicts with family, friends, workmates and so forth)
    - other past TRIGGERS.
- What are some possible TRIGGERS to look out for in future?
    - possible environmental TRIGGERS
    - possible interpersonal TRIGGERS
    - other possible TRIGGERS.

- What destructive behaviours and coping strategies has the client used in the past?
- What more constructive coping strategies has the client developed through the course of therapy?

In addition to identifying specific TRIGGERS, it is also important to compile a list of early warning signs that relapse is looming. For some clients, relapse is a very gradual process and there is no singular event *per se* that stands out as a TRIGGER. Often collections of factors are responsible for symptoms returning. Nipping relapse in the bud involves recognising subtle changes in mood, behaviour and thinking before they become more extreme and problematic. Below are some questions that can be used to this end:

- What early warnings signs may signal problems returning?
  - Consider: unhealthy negative emotions, mood variation, negative changes in thinking and behaviour.
- What lifestyle changes may indicate the risk of relapse?
  - Consider: work/life imbalance, withdrawal from social interaction, reduced communication/intimacy with significant others.
- What physical signs may alert the client to possible relapse?
  - Consider: sleep disturbance, increased/reduced appetite, lethargy and illness.

Once early warning signs have been explored, the next step is to refresh the client's memory about what has been most useful in treatment. Usually the strategies that helped the client to recover in the first place will work again in the event of a relapse:

- What areas does the client need to keep working on in order to maintain their therapeutic gains?
- Which specific CBT strategies aided the client most in overcoming their emotional/behavioural problems?

- What helpful beliefs and attitudes does the client need to continue practising and strengthening?
- What behavioural techniques has the client used to overcome their problems?
- Where can the client go for additional support if they start to struggle?
  - Consider: mental health professionals, GP, family members, friends and support groups.

Some clients may decide to resume regular CBT sessions if they are unable to emerge from a period of relapse independently. Alternatively, they may book a few 'top-up' sessions as a preventative measure. It is common practice for CBT therapists to include resumption of therapy in relapse prevention planning. Medication is also a consideration when dealing with relapse. If medication has helped in the past, it is prudent to encourage clients to keep an open mind about using it again if needed.

Endings

Treatment duration is discussed and negotiated from the beginning sessions and throughout CBT treatment. The regular review of goals and therapeutic progress keeps treatment on track and implies that it is time-limited rather than open-ended. Depending on the clinical setting, there may be a set amount of sessions available. In this case, the therapist may regularly remind the client how many sessions remain in order to make the best use of therapeutic time. Of course, relapse prevention planning in itself also addresses treatment conclusion. For these reasons, therapy termination is very much 'on the table' from the outset, steadily preparing the client for an end to regular sessions.

CBT's collaborative emphasis means that client and therapist work together as a team to help the client overcome their difficulties. As such, the client is an active participant in their own recovery and, through the acquisition of skills and techniques, effectively becomes their own therapist. Between-session practice via homework assignments increases client autonomy and self-efficacy. Indeed, the overall structure and implementation of CBT diminishes client dependency. Therefore endings do not come as a shock or a surprise to most CBT clients but are experienced as a natural progression. Generally, termination does not result in a particularly emotive response on the part of client or therapist. In fact, many CBT clients seem to prefer a business-like end to their treatment. Certainly CBT therapists exhibit appropriate warmth towards their clients when saying goodbye and many will express how rewarding it has been working with the client, if this is the case. Clients of CBT also will frequently offer thanks for the help they have received, but most clients will also recognise their own part in the process. In many cases, therapy endings are not unlike endings with any other service-providing professional.

That said, certain clients might find the prospect of leaving treatment more daunting than others. Common client concerns include worry that they won't be able to cope as well once treatment has ended and fears that they still have outstanding issues that may bring about relapse. In these instances, the CBT therapist will take special care with relapse prevention planning. Additionally, the therapist will strive to bolster client confidence and work gently but steadily on reducing client dependency on the therapeutic relationship. As we mentioned above, CBT therapists will generally be flexible (where possible) about when to end treatment, based on the client's circumstances and progress.

CBT clients are frequently offered 'top-up' sessions if this is deemed appropriate as part of their termination/relapse prevention plan. The client is urged to feel free to come back for a single session or series of sessions should they find themselves struggling any time post-treatment. As normal treatment progresses and the client becomes increasingly self-sufficient, sessions are tapered down to fortnightly, monthly or even longer intervals. This again prepares the client for a gradual arrival at permanent therapy termination and simultaneously leaves the door open for a resumption of sessions if and whenever necessary.

Chapter 10
Cognitive behaviour therapy transcript

CBT therapy is active-directive: that is, the therapist will ask direct questions with a view to building a conceptualisation of the client's difficulties from the very first session. While the client will, of course, be given space to ventilate and outline their difficulties, the CBT therapist will be listening with a keen ear and will help the client to see their problems more clearly within an ABC FRAMEWORK. This may be done overtly or more discreetly in the first session. The CBT therapist will endeavour to socialise the client to the CBT treatment protocol as early as appropriate by encouraging them to make a problem list and formulate associated goals to target during therapy sessions. In the first session, the CBT therapist will use core counselling skills such as active listening and reflecting to help build an alliance, but will also seek specific information and may even pose hypotheses about the client's emotional problems. Every initial session will vary in content and structure to some extent, based on the amount of information the therapist has received about the prospective client from the referral source; the severity of the client's problem; the level of training and experience of the CBT therapist, and the particular personality and communication style of both therapist and client.

Below is a transcript of a segment of an early CBT session. It is based on what actually took place in a real clinical session but has been changed so the client cannot be identified. As such, it is not an entirely verbatim transcript. Sections of the transcript are numbered (*T1*, *T2* and so forth) and the interventions the therapist is making at these points are explained.

It is an account of Melody's third session with a CBT therapist. She has been referred by her GP for ANXIETY in social situations that is affecting her university experience. Melody is meeting with her therapist (Martin) in an NHS surgery setting. In this segment, Martin sets an agenda for the session and looks in detail at a problem Melody experiences after having a positive social interaction. Melody is having treatment for social ANXIETY but also suffers with low mood. Together, she and Martin decide to focus on why she experiences a dip in mood after meeting with a friend.

Martin: Hi Melody, take a seat. There is some water there if you want some.

Melody: Thank you.

Martin: I'm going to check in on how you're doing and how you got on in the week. First, I'd like to do a quick mood check as usual. Could you rate how you think your mood has been on average this week?

T1: Martin has previously explained to Melody that they will conduct a mood check each session to establish a baseline level of her mood between sessions. A mood check is a very brief rating scale to quickly assess mood. In Melody's case, this is typically for depression. Each session Melody is encouraged to rate her mood between 1 and 10 – the higher the number the better her mood. This is in addition to disorder-specific measurement tools.

Melody: Umm... I'd say about a 4 on average, I think.

Martin: A 4, okay. So, about the same as the last couple of weeks.

Melody: Yeah, I've been kind of depressed the last couple of days...

Martin: Okay, we will talk about that. We also should look at the homework we set from the previous session, in particular how you have been doing regarding managing ANXIETY during social interactions.

T2: Each session incorporates building on between-session tasks or homework assignments. This is usually added as a specific agenda item, along with any other specific problems the client wishes to discuss. A piece of homework might be an ongoing way of behaving (or thinking) in a given situation, as opposed to a specific 'task' to do.

Martin: Is there anything else you also wanted to talk about specifically today?

Melody: No, not specifically, just my low mood.

Martin: Okay, do you want to start with that then?

Melody: Yeah, I guess so… I missed two seminars…

Martin: Because of…

Melody: I was away visiting my friends for one of them… but then the second time I was on my way and I bumped into a girl I sat next to last term and we stayed in the library instead…

Martin: Doing…?

Melody: We had a paper we were doing. We were sitting around and chatting…

Martin: That's good…

T3: Martin draws attention to a helpful behaviour that Melody engaged in – i.e. socialising in a public place. Melody had previously avoided doing this.

Melody: Yeah, it was good.

Martin: It sounds like it was a good use of time rather than going to the seminar, is that right?

T4: Martin validates Melody's decision not to attend the seminar and instead spend time practising small talk, which usually Melody finds very ANXIETY-provoking and avoids. As in T3 above, Martin takes every opportunity to provide appropriate praise when Melody engages in a positive behaviour. It is important to sincerely acknowledge small wins whenever they occur.

Melody: Yeah, yeah, and I guess I was feeling kind of depressed because I guess that happened and it went well, but then, not that it was over *per se*, but more that it was over and I was still in the same position as before. I wasn't just 'healed' after that.

Martin: What do you mean? In terms of social ANXIETY?

Melody: I guess so. I mean situationally. It's not a quick fix, that maybe I hoped it would be.

Martin: So maybe a bit disappointed that it didn't have more of a punch...

Melody: Yeah.

Martin: ... in terms of positive affect.

Melody: Yeah.

Martin: But during the conversation when you were chatting to this girl, are you able to rate your ANXIETY from 1–10?

Melody: I'd say between 1 and 5.

Martin: Can you be a bit more specific? Did it fluctuate between 1 and 5?

Melody: Yeah.

Martin: Okay, so that's not too bad? *(In the first sessions of treatment, Melody would have rated this much higher, at around 7 to 10)*

Melody: No, I suppose it is something of an improvement...

Martin: Can you remember when it hit a 5?

T5: Martin is enquiring about the most ANXIETY-provoking part of the interaction the client had with the classmate.

Melody: Yeah it was, I guess – I don't know specifically, but it was when two people aren't on the same page anymore, like when the conversation is getting on fine and then you misunderstand each other...

Martin: And you need to clarify and there is a bit of awkwardness?

T6: Martin is normalising aspects of the ANXIETY Melody felt during the interaction. Normalising helps the client understand that often how they feel is understandable and completely appropriate, which in turn helps them recognise normal, 'healthy' negative emotions.

Melody: Yeah, I think so.

Martin: That would make sense, wouldn't it. Those are the times when you would normally want to exit the situation. Am I right?

Melody: It was better than most situations because I had my laptop in front of me and any time it falls silent you can just look at it and you seem busy with something again, and that helps.

Martin: But, despite some trickier moments, you stuck with it, you didn't leave on a 5?

T7: Giving appropriate praise is essential for helping a client realise when they have made therapeutic progress. Here, Martin is offering praise for sticking with a difficult situation and reinforcing the idea that, when doing exposures, it is best not to leave an ANXIETY-provoking situation when ANXIETY is at its highest. Sticking with the exposure until there is a reduction in ANXIETY will demonstrate that ANXIETY decreases and Melody can tolerate it, and the next time she is faced with a similar situation, she will have a positive memory of coping.

Melody: Yeah, but I was nervous about how to leave when it came time. The seminar would have just ended and I would have just left, but I couldn't work out how to go about it…

Martin: Saying goodbye, parting ways?

Melody: Yeah, because there seems to be a tendency when you are leaving to give an explanation for why you are leaving.

Martin: How did that particular situation unfold? Can you describe how that leaving went?

Cognitive behaviour therapy transcript 105

Melody: Well, I had finished and just said, 'Right I'm leaving, I'm off.'

Martin: And she said...?

Melody: 'Okay, I'll see you later.' It was fine. But it's all in the anticipation, isn't it. I was sitting there thinking 'I've already had lunch; I can't say I'm off to get lunch.'

Martin: So, what did you say?

Melody I just said, 'I'm finished.'

Martin: So, you didn't really need to give her an explanation particularly... did you?

Melody: No, I just feel like you do have to explain, for some reason.

Martin: Okay... well, what did this experience show you about that?

Melody: Well, that you don't, I guess.

Martin: Yeah.

T8: Martin draws attention to evidence that is contradictory to Melody's idea that there is a social expectation to provide information as to why one leaves a situation. However, even though this was not the case on this occasion (as the person she was speaking to accepted her response), she could be faced with this problem in future. This is typically what causes some of her anticipatory ANXIETY. *Therefore, Martin will suggest ways to handle being asked the question she fears.*

Melody: I think what I'm more worried about is – well, in this case, yeah, it was okay, but I worry there are some situations where it's likely you'll go 'I'm off' and she will go 'How come?'

Martin: Yeah, what would be a reason you could give her if she did ask?

Melody: Well, sometimes you have a reason, but sometimes you want to leave just because you want to leave. Maybe you've just had enough.

Martin: Yeah...

Melody: ... and you want to go do something else or go home and be alone or something.

Martin: Yeah, so what would you say in that situation, do you think?

T9: Martin is encouraging Melody to entertain different verbal responses should the social interaction go the way she most fears.

Melody: I don't know, because isn't that kind of rude to say, 'I'm done with your company'?

Martin: Well, yeah that kind of would be... 'I've had enough of you I'm off...' (laughter). What do you think you could do or say instead?

T10: As in T9 above, Martin is encouraging Melody to come up with some possible alternative responses to being asked the question she fears. It is important that the therapist encourages the client to come up with their own alternative thoughts and ways of behaving so they can continue to do this post-therapy. Should these need to be adjusted or amended, the therapist can do this on hearing the response.

Melody: Umm... I don't know. Just make up some excuse like I have work to do or something.

Martin: Yeah... I'm going to go home to clean my room; I'm going to go meet someone else; I'm going to go have a rest; I'm going to go to the gym; I'm going to go practise communicating telepathically with my cat... do you know what I mean?

T11: Martin gives a ridiculous example to highlight the idea that any explanation will suffice and Melody is overthinking it.

Melody: Yeah.

Martin: Because I guess, sometimes, we tell a white lie, don't we, to end a social situation when we want to end it?

Melody: Yeah.

Martin: And how do you feel about that? Do you feel that is something you could do morally without guilt?

Melody: Yeah, I think so.

Martin: Yeah.

Melody: I think, typically though, I end up creating a story with lots of detail.

Martin: To try and make sure you don't get caught out or offend someone?

Melody: Yeah, like to make sure I don't go 'I'm off to get lunch' and then see them somewhere and they think I lied to get away from them or something like that, I guess.

Martin: Well, I understand that, but you are making a lot of assumptions about the other person's thoughts and feelings. Do you agree? Maybe a simple reason is the best option in the main?

Melody: Yeah, it would be more straightforward and then I can just go on my way.

Martin: Hmmm, yeah. Now let me just play devil's advocate here. What if you were 'off to get lunch', and they said they wanted to join you, what would happen inside you?

T12: Martin is encouraging Melody to entertain the worst-case scenario so that they can problem-solve this in the session and alleviate anticipatory ANXIETY *in the future. Envisaging the worst-case scenario with the client ensures that, should this actually happen, they will be able to tolerate and cope with it.*

Melody: Well, I would panic as I've never been to the eateries on campus, and at this stage it's embarrassing to admit that. I might not know how to order food.

Martin: It wouldn't be that complicated. You could work it out.

T13: Martin does not get side-tracked by a possible problem here. Instead, he subtly demonstrates he believes Melody is more than capable of entering a situation and behaving in a socially acceptable manner without knowing in advance the exact 'social rules'. It can be easy to get side-tracked by new or additional problems that the client presents. Staying focused ensures completion of the intervention started.

Melody: Right, yeah, but what if I did something wrong, and they are like 'What, you haven't been here before?'

Martin: And if you haven't?

Melody: I don't know. Then I'd have to explain why I'd never been there, and then I'd have to explain I've never really eaten with other people.

Martin: But it's about you deciding that you don't need to give a full explanation every time there is a social situation in life.

Melody: Yeah.

***T14**: Martin takes the opportunity to show Melody that she has already agreed it is socially and morally acceptable to tell a white lie.*

Martin: So, what is something else you might be able to say? There are a few things I can think of. Some of them might be tiny white lies and some of them might just be the truth.

***T15**: Martin encourages Melody to come up with her own responses rather than giving her the answers.*

Melody: I guess I could say, 'I just haven't.'

Martin: Yeah. 'I just haven't eaten here.'

Melody: Yeah.

Martin: 'I normally eat in my halls to save money', maybe – something like that.

Melody: I think the scenario I am worried about is if it becomes a friendly, jokey situation. Like if someone says, 'How have you not been to that cafe?' And for it to suddenly turn from light-hearted to being quite a miserable, depressing situation.

Martin: Well, why would it become a miserable depressing situation if it started out light-hearted?

T16: Martin is subtly helping Melody to see that her thinking can determine to what extent she feels depressed.

Melody: Well, if you are joking like that and then go, 'Oh well, I don't have any friends to eat with,' if you just jokingly said it like that.

Martin: Do you think it's going to bring everybody down?

T17: Melody has expressed this fear before, hence Martin hypothesises here.

Melody: Well, I think it could make people uncomfortable probably, not because they would be judging me but because they would potentially feel a bit sorry for me.

Martin: Well, if it did, if they did feel momentarily a bit awkward for having gotten something out of you that they think might be a sensitive issue, is it recoverable?

T18: Martin is assessing how bad Melody believes the situation would be, should the worst happen, and will then decide what to work on next – whether to help her to realise how it would be bearable or, if she agrees the situation is recoverable, then how to continue in the moment.

Melody: I suppose so. Yeah, it could be recovered.

Martin: So, what would you perhaps do to make it light-hearted again?

Melody: Make some joke about that?

Martin: Sure, or just change the subject?

Melody: Yeah, that is the most sensible solution.

Martin: See? You overthink it. You have two things going on: you have this fear of negative evaluation, right, and this fear of being pitied.

Melody: Yeah.

Martin: Is pitied the right word?

T19: *Martin checks to see if his assumption is correct and that Melody agrees this is true.*

Melody: Yeah, that's right, I can see that.

Martin: So that leads you to do what? When you think about going into these situations, what do you tend to do?

Melody: Well, overthink them, over-plan it.

Martin: Yeah, over-plan it. Spontaneity will come if you stop yourself from trying to anticipate every possible thing that might go wrong, because what you have seen, evidentially, is that there have been some moments that you haven't expected, and you haven't had time to think and plan and it's been alright, hasn't it?

Melody: Yeah, that's the thing. The other day on my way to the seminar, I was just walking down the stairs and I was late, and I was thinking 'Oh no, I need to go in there and sit next to people,' and I was getting nervous about that, and that girl just came round the corner on the stairs and asked me to go to the library. Because there was no time to get nervous about that, it was pretty much fine.

Martin: Okay, see, that's good, and I want you to really try and remember that, Melody, and to make notes of these successes, however small they may be, because that shows you that you are making progress.

T20: *Martin encourages Melody to make a note of any success as a between session or homework task.*

Summary

It is important to emphasise that this transcript represents only about 30 minutes of an actual session and is not representative of an entire therapeutic hour. It is also important to bear in mind that CBT doesn't always progress as quickly and smoothly as described here, although it can. While Melody stated she wanted to work on her low mood as the first agenda item, it became apparent that discussing the social interaction that she later became depressed about was an important topic that should not be overlooked. Points T1–T20 outline the specific skills or interactions that were present. Martin assessed the specific problem experienced by Melody (anticipatory ANXIETY caused by her tendency to over-plan a response), and set a between-session task of continuing to engage in small talk without planning a 'get out' in advance, to be acted on whenever Melody has the opportunity to do so.

Chapter 11
Applications and developments in cognitive behavioural therapy

Although widely used and accepted as efficacious for many years (Chapter 1 describes its history in more detail), CBT has become the main form of talking therapy on offer, certainly in the UK National Health Service.

In addition to its growing popularity in the UK, CBT is also widely practised in America, Canada and throughout Europe. Part of CBT's success is certainly due to its extensive evidence base. Its proven efficacy and relative brevity in comparison with other approaches make CBT an economical treatment strategy.

In 2008, in England, the Improving Access to Psychological Therapy (IAPT) service was introduced to provide government-funded, evidence-based psychological treatments for working-age adults with depression and ANXIETY disorders in primary care. The four defining features of IAPT are:

1. It offers NICE-approved, time-limited, evidence-based psychological therapies delivered by trained practitioners.
2. It follows a 'stepped-care' model of incremental intensity, starting with 'low intensity' guided self-help and progressing to 'high intensity' one-to-one talking therapies.
3. Providers are required to complete and report routine outcome monitoring

4. Its practitioners receive regular, outcomes-focused supervision.

IAPT aims to progressively increase its capacity to provide talking therapy to some 1.9 million people in England by 2024 (NHS England, 2019): from 15% of people with ANXIETY and depression per year to 25% (BABCP, 2019). There are also plans to provide talking therapy for people diagnosed with long-term medical conditions.

This is probably the single biggest step forward in the provision of talking therapies that we have ever seen in the UK. It means that mental health is now recognised by the government as a major issue for our times, and something that requires and responds to early primary care intervention.

Psychological therapies, such as CBT, have proved to be as effective as drugs in tackling common mental health problems and are often more effective in the longer term. NICE, the national body responsible for assessing and publishing guidelines on health and social care treatments in England, recommends talking therapies such as CBT for treating ANXIETY and depression (NICE, 2009).

Psychiatric conditions

Increasingly, CBT is being cited as the psychological intervention best used for treating a number of common psychiatric conditions. CBT is specifically indicated in the NICE guidelines for treatment of the following disorders:

- generalised ANXIETY disorder (GAD)
- ANXIETY disorders, including social phobia, panic, agoraphobia and other phobias
- depression
- illness ANXIETY disorder (health ANXIETY)
- post-traumatic stress disorder (PTSD)
- body dysmorphic disorder (BDD)
- OBSESSIVE-COMPULSIVE DISORDER (OCD)

- anorexia, bulimia and atypical eating disorders
- chronic fatigue syndrome
- insomnia
- irritable bowel syndrome
- schizophrenia
- long-term conditions such as chronic pain.

CBT is also being adapted and offered to a growing variety of populations. While efficacy in these populations is less well researched, CBT is being offered to:

- older adults
- children and young people
- black, Asian and minority ethic people
- women with perinatal and postnatal ANXIETY and depressive disorders.

CBT 'waves'

Classical CBT (REBT and CT) is often referred to as 'second wave' COGNITIVE behaviour therapies, following on from the 'first wave' behaviour therapies of the 1950s and 1960s. More and more new therapies based on CBT theory and principles have been developed over recent years. Many of these are creating evidence bases of their own. Some of these newer forms of CBT, such as acceptance and commitment therapy (ACT), are referred to as 'third wave' CBT. There is not space to go into great depth about these therapies in this chapter. However the more prominent ones are:

- mindfulness-based COGNITIVE therapy (MBCT) – based on CBT principles and mindfulness meditation, this approach has been found effective for depression. For more information, read *Full Catastrophe Living* by Jon Kabat-Zinn (2013)
- schema-focused therapy (SFT) – developed by Jeffery Young, this approach focuses on the treatment of personality disorders

- acceptance and commitment therapy (ACT) – Steven Haynes is the foremost expert on ACT. This approach has been used to treat chronic pain and emotional disorders. You can find out more on the Association for Contextual and Behavioural Science website at https://contextualscience.org
- behavioural activation (BA) – this approach has proved highly effective for the treatment of depression. To find out more, read *Behavioural Activation for Depression: A clinician's guide* (Martell et al., 2010)
- dialectical behaviour therapy (DBT) – this was developed by Marsha Linehan in the late 1980s for the treatment of people with a diagnosis of borderline personality disorder (BPD). While similar to CBT in many ways, DBT emphasises psychosocial aspects of treatment and usually involves both individual and group therapy
- compassion-focused therapy (CFT) – a multimodal therapy that builds on aspects of CBT as well as a range of other modalities. In addition to focusing on attention, COGNITION, behaviour and emotions, it incorporates compassion-focused imagery, mindfulness, psychoeducation on the CFT model and compassionate self-correction, to name a few. For more information, read Paul Gilbert's *The Compassionate Mind* (2010).

There is now talk of a 'fourth wave' (Peteet, 2018) that is said to look beyond traditional CBT foci such as insight, mastery and problem-solving specific dysfunctions and disorders, and toward the achievement of positive wellbeing. US psychiatrist John Peteet (Peteet, 2018) posits that this fourth wave builds on CBT's insistence that the client always remains the central player in their own recovery, and lists under this fourth-wave umbrella positive psychology interventions, loving kindness and compassion mediation, and dignity-and-gratitude-promoting, meaning-centred, forgiveness-oriented and spiritually informed therapies. He also sees some overlap with formal spiritual/religious practices such as prayer and supportive communities, which all have some role in helping people 'flourish'.

Settings

CBT is practised in private and NHS hospitals, in groups and one-to-one. Increasingly, mental health nurses are being encouraged to take further training in CBT. Voluntary sector counselling services also now offer CBT. Many charity-run alcohol and drug rehabilitation units are using CBT either in conjunction with or instead of the traditional 12-step approach.

There are numerous CBT self-help books on the market that clients can read to find out more about CBT, help themselves overcome problems or use in conjunction with professional CBT treatment.

Computerised and online CBT

Computerised and online CBT are becoming increasingly popular and available. There are many CBT apps available for individuals to use either alongside treatment or as self-help (e.g. Mood Kit[1] and iMood[2]) and for organisations to use to provide support to service users and employees (e.g. What's Up?[3]). A growing number of applications are being developed for specific disorders that people can use via their mobile phones, tablets or computers.

Computerised CBT

A number of digital mental healthcare providers have developed online guided self-help programmes based on CBT principles and practice. Users complete specific modules relevant to the problems they are experiencing (e.g. depression). These programmes can be completed as an adjunct to therapy, as guided self-help or as a firstline treatment when accessing IAPT services.

Online/remote therapy

There has been a growing trend for CBT therapists in both the

---

1. www.thriveport.com/products/moodkit
2. www.imoodjournal.com
3. www.thewhatsupapp.co.uk

private and NHS sectors to provide CBT therapy online. This is different from the online modules discussed above, as these are CBT sessions carried out (typically) via video (or phone, asynchronous email or instant messaging) between the CBT therapist and client. It is not uncommon for CBT therapists to occasionally provide a therapy session via video call but to conduct the majority of sessions face to face. However, due to the limited availability of CBT therapists in some areas, the high demand for therapy, and long waiting lists, and also most recently the Covid-19 pandemic and consequent lockdowns, there has been a move towards more use of online therapy services. Online sessions can also enable continuity of care when clients move house during treatment, or need post-therapy follow-up.

There are now many therapy agencies that CBT therapists can join that exclusively provide online therapy.

A list of accredited CBT therapists is available from the British Association for Behavioural and Cognitive Psychotherapies (BABCP) website. The British Association for Counselling and Psychotherapy (BACP) also has an online directory of its members, including those offering CBT, as does the National Counselling Society (NCS). These practitioners will all be registered with the national voluntary registration scheme (the Professional Standards Authority (PSA)), and will list in their directory entries where they are based and what they offer, the modalities they use and any areas of specialist practice. Website details for these organisations can be found in Appendix 1.

Chapter 12
Research into cognitive behaviour therapy

COGNITIVE behaviour therapy is probably the most researched of all the psychotherapy models. In fact, it is so well researched that it becomes difficult to decide what to include in one short chapter. We have therefore opted to simply give an overview of current research on CBT efficacy for some of the common mental disorders and some specific population groups.

Proven efficacy

CBT is perhaps best known for its effectiveness in the treatment of depression and ANXIETY disorders. As has already been mentioned in the previous chapter, NICE recommends CBT as the preferred psychological intervention in its treatment guidelines for a number of psychiatric diagnoses. In order for NICE to authorise a specific treatment, the approach needs to be proven effective through randomised controlled trials. This speaks to the scientific rigour that CBT research has managed to achieve, and the fact that this manualised approach lends itself well to the methodology of randomised controlled trials. Research into the effectiveness of CBT for many different types of disorders continues. The incorporation of emerging research results into existing theory and practice keeps CBT a vibrant and contemporary therapy.

CBT for anxiety disorders

The efficacy of CBT for ANXIETY disorders is well documented and research into specific interventions with a wide range of populations such as young people, older adults and people with learning difficulties continues to grow. A meta-analysis conducted by Olatunji and colleagues (2010) demonstrates that CBT procedures (particularly exposure-based approaches) are highly efficacious in the treatment of ANXIETY disorders. They conclude that CBT generally outperforms placebo and waiting list controls and tends also to outperform other psychosocial treatment modalities.

There is a vast body of research that has evaluated the effectiveness of CBT for panic disorder and agoraphobia. CBT has been proved cost effective and quick acting, and to have long-term maintenance and treatment benefits for panic disorder (Otto & Deveney, 2005). The effects of CBT treatment are usually sustained over time (Barlow, 2014) and booster (topup) sessions further enhance its long-term outcomes (Craske et al., 2006).

CBT for social ANXIETY typically comprises correcting COGNITIVE biases, restructuring unhealthy CORE BELIEFS where necessary, and making use of behavioural experiments and exposures to erode negative beliefs and strengthen healthy alternatives. CT for social ANXIETY, in particular a package of exposure and COGNITIVE RESTRUCTURING techniques, is an effective intervention for the treatment of social ANXIETY and has shown superior results to interpersonal therapy (Barlow, 2014).

Generalised ANXIETY disorder remains one of the least successfully treated ANXIETY disorders, with evidence to suggest that less than 65% of those receiving treatment recover sufficiently to be rated as high functioning (Newman et al., 2011). Despite this, there are a number of meta-analyses showing that COGNITIVE behavioural therapies are efficacious and achieve large effect sizes that persist over follow-up periods (Covin et al., 2008). Exposure is widely considered an effective intervention in the treatment of specific phobia (such as animal phobia, dental phobia, emetophobia and so forth). Ost (1997) demonstrated that a single, long session of exposure treatment can yield good results. Riddle-Walker and colleagues (2016) found CBT to be significantly more effective for people with emetophobia than being assigned to a waiting list. For more information on the effectiveness of CBT for ANXIETY disorders, *Cognitive Therapy for Anxiety Disorders* (Simos & Hofmann, 2013) is an excellent resource.

Obsessive-compulsive disorders (OCDs)

Behavioural interventions and their efficacy in the treatment of OCD have been well researched since the 1960s. CBT treatment for OCD has been refined over the last few decades and it has since become the most efficacious form of therapy for this condition. Meta-analyses demonstrate that exposure and response prevention – a form of CBT treatment for OCD – is an effective firstline intervention, and that, when combined with COGNITIVE therapy, may improve adherence to treatment and tolerance of distress and reduce drop-out (McKay et al., 2015).

Disorders such as body dysmorphic disorder (BDD), trichotillomania and hoarding are categorised as 'obsessive-compulsive and related disorders' in *DSM-5* (APA, 2013), meaning they are no longer considered sub-types of OCD (as they were in *DSM-IV*) (APA, 2004) but as disorders in their own right. Many of the evidenced-based approaches to treating OCD are also effective with these disorders. Harrison and colleagues (2016) found CBT to be efficacious for BDD, that gains are maintained 2–4 months post-treatment, and that CBT treatment for BDD also improves related features of the disorder, such as depression and insight. For a detailed examination of CBT for BDD, *Overcoming Obsessive-Compulsive Disorder* (Veale & Neziroglu, 2010) is recommended.

CBT for trichotillomania has shown promising results. Specifically, interventions known as habit-reversal training are particularly effective, although relapse is common (Franklin et al., 2011).

A systematic review (Williams & Viscusi, 2016) has established that symptoms of hoarding disorder are improved with the use of CBT interventions designed for treatment of OCD. However, the researchers stress the need for further research in this specialist area. For a detailed review of which aspects of CBT treatment are effective, we recommend Franklin and Foa's chapter (Franklin & Foa, 2014) on OCD in the *Clinical Handbook of Psychological Disorders: A step by step treatment manual* (Barlow, 2014).

Post-traumatic stress disorder (PTSD)

CBT treatment for PTSD is well researched. Variations of CBT such as prolonged exposure therapy (PE) and COGNITIVE processing therapy (CPT) have been proven highly effective in reducing symptoms. According to Rauch and colleagues (2010), PE has been subject to many clinical trials that have demonstrated its efficacy. They argue that, where risk of harm (from self or others) is low, PE should be considered an essential part of the PTSD treatment plan. CPT, an approach developed by Patricia Resick and colleagues, has been shown to be highly effective in reducing PTSD in combat veterans, victims of sexual assault and people caught up in natural disasters. CPT can be delivered individually or in groups.

For a detailed review of CPT and its supporting evidence, read Resick and colleagues' *Cognitive Processing Therapy for PTSD: A comprehensive manual* (2017). For an overview of CBT treatment for OCD, we recommend Rachman's paper, 'The evolution of behaviour therapy and cognitive behaviour therapy' (2015).

Depression

Aaron Beck wrote the comprehensive text *Depression: Clinical, experimental and theoretical aspects* in 1967. Since then, CBT interventions for depression, whether CT, CBT or behavioural approaches such as behavioural activation/behavioural activation treatment for depression, are probably the most widely researched among all CBT approaches for any one disorder. That said, depression itself is a complex problem and treatment outcomes for particular types of depression (i.e. major depressive disorder, persistent depressive disorder, cyclothymia and so forth) vary. Broadly speaking, CBT treatment for unipolar and bipolar depression has been shown to benefit adolescents and older people (Barlow, 2014). However, a meta-analysis by Johnsen and Friborg (2015) found CBT to be not quite as successful in the treatment of depression as it once was, and they suggest this could be due to several factors, including poor-quality training of therapists and a misconception that CBT is easy to learn. As mentioned in Chapter 7, behavioural activation is effective in reducing symptoms of severe depression and is an area of CBT currently receiving much interest.

CBT for specific populations

Older adults

CBT is recommended for older people suffering from common mental health problems such as those listed above. Depression, ANXIETY disorders and chronic pain are commonly experienced by older adults and there is evidence to suggest CBT can help alleviate symptoms. A metanalysis conducted by Kishita and Laidlaw (2017) found CBT had moderate effects in older adults with generalised ANXIETY disorder (GAD) and suggest a need for age-appropriate CBT for those suffering from ANXIETY and depression later in life. Cox and D'Oyley (2011) found that both COGNITIVE therapy and behavioural therapy were significantly more effective than placebo for depression among older people and for relapse prevention of mood disorders. There is a welcome increase in research into CBT and its efficacy in this population, but further research is required to demonstrate how it may best be adapted to their specific needs.

LGBTQI+

CBT 'for' lesbian, gay, bisexual, transgender, queer, intersex, pansexual, non-binary and asexual people (who in this book we refer to as LGBTQI+) is a misnomer, as diversity in sexual identity is very much not a disorder. Treatment aimed at changing a person's sexual orientation is banned under the ethical codes of all the main psy professions, but unfortunately is still inflicted all too commonly on the LGBQI+ community across the world. While talking therapy in some cases may focus on internalised homophobia, more often it is focused on issues that this community shares with the rest of humanity, such as social ANXIETY, depression and so on, and indeed is more vulnerable to. CBT therapists need to be aware that LGBTQI+ clients may have faced discrimination, violence, prejudice, rejection when coming out and difficulties forming romantic relationships, in particular after decades of denying their feelings and identifying as heterosexual.

Therapists should have an understanding of the many types of 'non-traditional' family structures and the impacts of oppression and discrimination due to age, ethnicity and religion. Research suggests that many healthcare professionals have very limited knowledge about LGBTQI+ health issues (Guasp & Taylor, 2012). For more information on CBT for LGBTQI+ clients, we recommend *Cognitive-Behavioural Therapies with Lesbian, Gay and Bisexual Clients* (Martell et al., 2004) and *Mindfulness and Acceptance for Gender and Sexual Minorities* (Skinta & Curtin, 2016).

Black, Asian and minority ethnic people

CBT was developed and has subsequently been refined by therapists and trainers who are typically from religious, ethnic and sexual majorities – in other words, Christian, white and heterosexual. Therefore the efficacy of CBT for black, Asian and minority ethnic people cannot be assumed from studies unless they specifically state the ethnicities of the subjects, which few if any do. Adapting CBT to meet different cultural needs while still adhering to CBT evidence-based principles is a difficult undertaking but is an area of significant interest (Stone et al., 2018). For an overview of the cultural adaptation of CBT for black, Asian and ethnic minority communities and its application with other social and cultural minority groups, we recommend the January 2019 special issue of *The Cognitive Behaviour Therapist* (Thwaite, 2019).

Where to find out more

For up-to-date research papers on CBT, the international journal *Behavioural and Cognitive Psychotherapy*, published by Cambridge University Press, is an excellent resource.

Appendix 1
Resources for learning

Organisations

Albert Ellis Institute (AEI) – www.albertellisinstitute.org

Association for Contextual Behavioural Science (ACBS) – www.contextualpsychology.org

British Association for Behavioural and Cognitive Psychotherapies (BABCP) – www.babcp.com

British Association for Counselling and Psychotherapy (BACP) – www.bacp.co.uk

National Counselling Society (NCS) – https://nationalcounsellingsociety.org

National Institute for Health and Care Excellence (NICE) – www.nice.org.uk

CBT training

The majority of CBT training courses in the UK now come under the remit of the NHS, meaning those wishing to train in CBT are more likely to find a course provided by the NHS, through a university. These courses provide postgraduate diplomas in 'High Intensity Therapy (HIT)'. Courses independent of the NHS provide postgraduate diplomas in CBT. Both routes are currently accredited by the BABCP.

Further reading

Bennett-Levy, J., Butler, G., Fennell, M., Hackman, A., Mueller, M. & Westbrook, D. (Eds.) (2004). *Oxford guide to behavioural experiments in cognitive therapy*. Oxford University Press.

Burns, D.D. (2000). *The feeling good handbook* (2nd revised ed.). Plume.

Constable & Robinson. *The Overcoming Series*. https://overcoming.co.uk

Dryden, W. (ed.) (2007). *Dryden's handbook of individual therapy* (5th ed.). Sage.

Martell, C.R., Dimidjian, S. & Herman-Dunn, R. (2013). *Behavioural activation for depression: A clinician's guide*. Guilford Press.

Neenan, M. & Dryden, W. (2004). *Cognitive therapy: 100 key points*. Brunner Routledge.

Wells, A. (1997). *Cognitive behaviour therapy for anxiety disorders*. Wiley.

Willson, R. & Branch, R. (2020). *Cognitive behavioural therapy for dummies*. Wiley.

Websites and online CBT self-help programmes

Beating the Blues offers online CBT courses for both therapists and those looking to manage depression and anxiety – www.beatingtheblues.co.uk

Mood Gym teaches CBT techniques for overcoming depression and anxiety – www.moodgym.anu.edu.au

No Panic offers advice and support for all types of anxiety disorders – www.nopanic.org.uk

Appendix 2
Relapse prevention worksheet

Overview of problems and goals
What were the original presenting problems that brought me to treatment (e.g. emotional, behavioural, interpersonal, practical problems; psychiatric diagnosis)?
What goals were set in relation to these problems?
What goal-directed changes have I made thus far?
What are the benefits of the therapeutic changes or progress I have made thus far?

Review of belief change	
What negative core beliefs were identified?	What healthy alternative core beliefs have been established/ strengthened during treatment?
Self: Others: World:	Self: Others: World:
What maladaptive assumptions/ rules have been identified?	What adaptive or alternative assumptions/rules have been developed?
What thinking errors do I or did I typically engage in (e.g. mind-reading, personalising, black-and-white thinking)? Include some examples.	
What realistic interpretations do I now have to counteract the thinking errors listed above?	
What skills have I learned to enable me to 'answer back' and to challenge my negative automatic thoughts?	

Recognising triggers

What types of situations or conditions have typically triggered unhealthy core beliefs/maladaptive assumptions/NATs?

Past environmental triggers (e.g. illness, financial, work stress etc.)	Past interpersonal triggers (e.g. relationship conflicts with family, friends, colleagues etc.)

Other possible triggers:

What destructive behaviours and coping strategies have I used/did I use in the past?

What are more constructive coping strategies that I have developed through the course of therapy?

Early warning signs

What early warning signs may signal my problems are returning (consider unhealthy negative emotions, mood variation, negative changes in thinking and behaviour)?

What lifestyle changes may indicate the risk of relapse (consider work/life balance, withdrawal from social interaction, reduced communication/intimacy with significant others)?

What physical signs may alert me to possible relapse (consider difficulties sleeping, increased/reduced tiredness, illness etc.)?

What has been most useful throughout therapy?
What areas specifically do I need to keep working on to maintain the gains I've made?

What specific behavioural techniques do I need to continue to do (consider exposures undertaken in therapy, new behaviours I should continue to reinforce)?

Where can I go for additional support if I start to struggle?

Glossary

ABC FORMAT/FRAMEWORK/MODEL – A structured format used throughout CBT therapies where 'A' represents a TRIGGER EVENT, 'B' represents thoughts and beliefs and 'C' represents emotional, COGNITIVE and behavioural responses.

ACTIVATING EVENT – An event, either external or internal, actual or perceived, that triggers underlying beliefs and results in an emotional response. Represented as 'A' in the ABC FORMAT.

ADAPTIVE ALTERNATIVE ASSUMPTIONS – Immediate thoughts in response to ambiguous or negative events based on personal rules for living. ADAPTIVE ASSUMPTIONS are functional in that they lead to constructive behaviour. These are developed through therapy to replace pre-existing MALADAPTIVE ASSUMPTIONS that perpetuate emotional disturbance and destructive behaviour.

ADAPTIVE BEHAVIOUR   A constructive behaviour (or change in behaviour) enabling adjustment to circumstance.

ADAPTIVE COGNITION – Thoughts that promote healthy emotional responses and adjustment to aversive events.

AFFECT LADEN – Emotionally charged aspects of an individual's thoughts or experiences.

ALLIANCE CONCEPTS – Ideas and principles related to the therapeutic relationship.

ANXIETY – An emotional response when faced with real or perceived threat, risk or danger.

ATTENTIONAL BIAS – The tendency to focus on one or more aspects of a given situation to the exclusion of all other aspects.

AVERSIVE EMOTIONS – Extreme or inappropriate emotional responses to events that impede problem-solving and overall ability to function effectively.

AVOIDANCE – The desire or tendency to avoid thoughts, situations or events that are likely to give rise to uncomfortable emotions and/or physiological responses.

BEHAVIOURISM – A school of OBJECTIVE psychology and philosophy that rejects SUBJECTIVE EXPERIENCE and consciousness. It states that the only relevant, valid psychological events are those that can be observed – i.e. behaviour.

CASE CONCEPTUALISATION – The process of collecting information from the client and building a picture of their problems using elements of the ABC FRAMEWORK.

CLASSICAL CONDITIONING – A process of behaviour modification using an unconditioned stimulus and a conditioned stimulus to produce a conditioned response. Using Pavlov's experiment as an example, food (unconditioned stimulus) produces salivation (unconditioned response). After repetition of combining food with the sound of a bell, the bell becomes a conditioned stimulus eliciting salivation (conditioned response).

COGNITION – The mental action of acquiring knowledge through perception and experience. Any type of thought is a COGNITION.

COGNITIVE – Refers to the process of thinking.

COGNITIVE DISSONANCE – The state of having inconsistent thoughts, beliefs or attitudes, especially relating to behavioural decisions and attitude change.

COGNITIVE RESTRUCTURING – The process of helping a client to change their thinking and belief systems in order to promote psychological health.

COGNITIVE VARIABLES – Mental activity that accounts for variations in psychological, emotional and behavioural responses.

COLLABORATIVE EMPIRICISM – The process of client and therapist working together to gather evidence for and against a specific client belief.

CONDITIONING – To train or accustom an animal or human being to respond in a prescribed manner when confronted with a specific stimulus. See also CLASSICAL CONDITIONING and OPERANT CONDITIONING.

CONGRUENCE – One of the CORE CONDITIONS postulated by Carl Rogers. In CBT, therapist verbal and non-verbal behaviours are consistent with the message they wish to impart to the client.

CORE BELIEFS – Deeply held beliefs that inform an individual's understanding of themselves, other people and the world around them.

CORE CONDITIONS – Elements of the therapeutic relationship deemed necessary and sufficient to promote therapeutic change, as postulated by Carl Rogers. These form the basis of person-centred therapy.

CORE SCHEMATA – See CORE BELIEFS.

COUNTERTRANSFERENCE – The emotional response of the counsellor to a client in psychodynamic therapy.

DIDACTIC TEACHING – The psycho-educational component of CBT. The therapist explicitly sets out to educate the client about core principles of CBT.

DISPUTATION – The process of using empirical, logical and pragmatic arguments to encourage the client to reassess the validity of their problematic beliefs.

EMPATHY – The ability to understand and share the feelings of another person. One of the CORE CONDITIONS postulated by Carl Rogers.

HABITUATION – The diminishing of a psychological or emotional response through frequent exposure to a stimulus.

INFERENTIAL – Refers to conclusions made on the basis of reasoning and gathering evidence. In CBT terms, client inferences may be faulty due to the influence of MALADAPTIVE ASSUMPTIONS and CORE SCHEMATA.

INTERACTIONALISM – Refers to reciprocal action and influence between actual events, COGNITIVE processes and emotions.

IRRATIONAL BELIEFS – Personal demands that certain conditions must exist. IRRATIONAL BELIEFS are postulated by Albert Ellis to underpin all types of emotional and psychological disturbance. See also RATIONAL BELIEFS.

LIKERT SCALE – A scale used in the sciences to measure spectrum-based phenomena. Generally constructed from 0–10 where 0 represents the extreme low end of the spectrum and 10 represents the extreme high end.

MALADAPTIVE ASSUMPTIONS – See ADAPTIVE ALTERNATIVE ASSUMPTIONS.

MALADAPTIVE BEHAVIOUR – Counterproductive behaviour (or change in behaviour) that impedes adjustment to circumstances.

NEGATIVE AUTOMATIC THOUGHTS (NATS) – Negative and self-defeating thoughts that seem to spontaneously occur in response to an ACTIVATING EVENT.

OBJECTIVE – Impartially considering and representing the facts of an event without being influenced by personal feelings or beliefs.

OBSESSIVE-COMPULSIVE DISORDER (OCD) – A psychiatric condition characterised by obsessive intrusive thoughts and/or compulsive performance of ritualistic behaviour.

OPERANT CONDITIONING – A process of behaviour modification conditioned through positive or negative reinforcement, and largely determined by consequences.

PRIMARY PREVENTION RESEARCH – Research looking at the factors that predispose people to certain conditions/distress, such as social and environmental conditions and personal characteristics and experiences.

PSYCHOANALYSIS/PSYCHOANALYTIC – School of psychology originated by and based on the work of Sigmund Freud.

PSYCHOPATHOLOGY – The study or manifestation of mental (psychological) disorder (pathology). A term originating in the medicalisation of distress.

QUALITATIVE (concept) – An idea relating to a quality that cannot be measured precisely. For example, a red ball, a happy occasion, a frightening experience.

QUANTITATIVE (concept) – An idea relating to a quality that can be measured precisely. For example, six inches of rain, a temperature of 92 degrees.

RATIONAL BELIEFS – Personal preferences that certain conditions ideally exist. RATIONAL BELIEFS lead to healthy psychological adjustment and emotional responses if conditions are not met. See also IRRATIONAL BELIEFS.

RECONCEPTUALISATION – The process of reviewing an original CASE CONCEPTUALISATION and refining it in light of new information. See also CASE CONCEPTUALISATION.

SAFETY BEHAVIOURS/STRATEGIES – Behaviours and methods used by the client to prevent activating uncomfortable emotions and psychological responses.

SOCRATIC QUESTIONING – The process of using questions to encourage clients to think for themselves, thereby guiding them towards a therapeutically relevant conclusion.

SUBJECTIVE EXPERIENCE – The understanding of a personal experience based on idiosyncratic beliefs, thoughts and emotions. (Dependant on personal perception.)

THERAPEUTIC ALLIANCE – The quality of the professional relationship between therapist and client. See also CORE CONDITIONS.

THINKING BIASES – The tendency to repeatedly think in ways consistent with an underlying belief about the self, others and the world. Also refers to faulty information processing.

THOUGHT–FEELING LINK/INTERACTION – Refers to the mutually reinforcing relationship between thoughts and emotions.

TRANSFERENCE – The process whereby a client imputes thoughts and feelings in the therapist that actually refer to previous important figures (usually parents) in the client's life.

TRIGGERS – See ACTIVATING EVENTS.

UNCONDITIONAL POSITIVE REGARD – One of the CORE CONDITIONS postulated by Carl Rogers. The therapist maintains a non-judgemental and accepting attitude toward the client.

References

American Psychiatric Association (APA). (2004). *Diagnostic and statistical manual of mental disorders-IV-TR* (4th ed. text revision). American Psychiatric Association.

American Psychiatric Association (APA). (2013). *Diagnostic and statistical manual of mental disorders* (5th ed.). American Psychiatric Association.

BABCP (2019). *BABCP response to the NHS 10-year plan*. https://www.babcp.com/About/News-Press/BABCP-Response-to-the-NHS-10-Year-Plan

Bandura, A. (1977a). *Social learning theory*. Prentice Hall.

Bandura, A. (1977b). Self-efficacy toward a unifying theory of behavioural change. *Psychological Review, 84*(2), 191–215.

Barlow, D.H. (Ed.). (2014). *Clinical handbook of psychological disorders: A step by step treatment manual* (5th ed.). Guilford Press.

Beck, A.T. (1967). *Depression: Clinical, experimental and theoretical aspects*. Harper and Row.

Beck, A.T. (1976). *Cognitive therapy and the emotional disorders*. Penguin.

Beck, A.T., Rush, A.J., Shaw, B.F. & Emery, G. (1979). *Cognitive therapy of depression*. Guilford Press.

Beck, J. (2011). *Cognitive therapy: Basics and beyond*. Guilford Press.

Burns, D.D. (1990). *The feeling good handbook*. Plume/Penguin.

Clark, D.M. (1986). A cognitive approach to panic. *Behavioural research and therapy, 24*(4), 461–470.

Clark D.M., Beck, A.T. & Alford, B.A. (1999). Scientific foundations of cognitive behaviour therapy. Oxford University Press.

Covin, R., Ouimet, A.J., Seeds, P.M. & Dozois, D.J.A. (2008). A meta-analysis of CBT for pathological worry among clients with GAD. *Journal of Anxiety Disorders, 22*(1),108–116.

Cox, D. & D'Oyley, H. (2011). Cognitive behavioural therapy with older adults. *Medical Journal, 53*(7), 348–352.

Craske, M.G., Roy-Byrne, P., Stein, M.B., Sullivan, G., Hazlett-Stevens, H., Bystritsky, A. & Sherbourne, C. (2006). CBT intensity and outcome for panic disorder in a primary care setting. *Behavior Therapy, 37*(2), 112–119.

Davies, E. & Burdett, J. (2004). Preventing 'schizophrenia': Creating the conditions for saner societies. In J. Read, L.R. Mosher & R.P. Bentall (Eds.), *Models of madness: Psychological, social and biological approaches to schizophrenia.* (pp. 271–282). Routledge.

Dionigi, A. & Canestrari, C. (2018). The use of humour by therapists and clients in cognitive therapy. *European Journal of Humour Research, 6*(3), 50. http://doi.org/10.7592/EJHR2018.6.3.dionigi

Dobson, K.S. & Block, L. (1988). Historical and philosophical bases of the cognitive behavioral therapies. In K.S. Dobson (Ed.), *Handbook of cognitive behavioral therapies* (pp. 3–38). Guilford Press.

Dryden, W. (2021). The rational emotive behaviour therapy primer. PCCS Books.

Dryden, W. & Branch, R. (2008). *Fundamentals of rational emotive behaviour therapy.* Wiley.

Dryden, W. & Branch, R. (Eds.). (2012). *The CBT handbook.* Sage.

Ellis, A. (1994) *Reason and emotion in psychotherapy: A comprehensive method of treating human disturbances.* Birch Lane Press.

Ellis, A (2005). Science and philosophy: Comparison of cognitive therapy and rational emotive behaviour therapy. *Journal of Cognitive Psychotherapy, 19*(2), 181–185.

Franklin, M.E. & Foa, E.B. (2014). Obsessive-compulsive disorder. In D.H. Barlow (Ed.), *Clinical handbook of psychological disorders: A step by step treatment manual* (5th ed.) (pp.155–205). Guilford Press.

Franklin, M.E., Zagrabbe, K. & Benavides, K.L. (2011). Trichotillomania and its treatment: A review and recommendations. *Expert Review of Neurotherapeutics, 11*(8), 1165–1174.

Gilbert, P. (2010). *The compassionate mind.* Constable & Robinson.

Gilbert, P. & Leahy, R.L. (Eds.). (2007). *The therapeutic relationship in cognitive behavioural psychotherapies.* Routledge.

Guasp, A. & Taylor, J. (2012). *Domestic abuse: Stonewall health briefing.* Stonewall

Hackman, A. (1998). Cognitive therapy with panic and agoraphobia: Working with complex cases. In N. Tarrier, A. Wells & G. Haddock (Eds.),

Treating complex cases: The cognitive behavioural therapy approach (pp. 27–45). Wiley.

Harrison, A., Fernandez de la Crus, L., Enander, J., Radua, J. & Mataix-Cols, D. (2016). Cognitive-behavioral therapy for body dysmorphic disorder: A systematic review and meta-analysis of randomized controlled trials. *Clinical Psychology Review, 48,* 43–51.

Hope, D.A., Heimberg, R.G. & Turk, C.L. (2010). *Managing social anxiety: A cognitive behavioural therapy approach. Therapist guide.* Oxford University Press.

Hopko, D.R., Lejuez, C.W., Ruggiero, K.J. & Eifert, G.H. (2003). Contemporary behavioral activation treatments for depression: Procedures, principles, and progress. *Clinical Psychology Review, 23*(5), 699–717.

Jacobson, N.S., Dobson, K.S., Truax, P.A., Addis, M.E., Koerner, K., Gollan, J.K., Gortner, E. & Prince, S.E. (1996). A component analysis of cognitive-behavioral treatment for depression. *Journal of Consulting and Clinical Psychology, 64*(2), 295–304.

Johnsen, T.J. & Friborg, O. (2015). The effects of cognitive behavioural therapy as an anti-depressive treatment is falling: A meta-analysis. *Psychological Bulletin, 141*(4), 747–768.

Kabat-Zinn, J. (2013). *Full catastrophe living: How to cope with stress, pain and illness using mindfulness meditation* (Revised ed.). Piatkus.

Kanter, J.W., Busch, A.M. & Rusch, L.C. (2009). *Behavioural activation: Distinctive features.* Routledge.

Kishita, N. & Laidlaw, K. (2017). Cognitive behaviour therapy for generalized anxiety disorder: Is CBT equally efficacious in adults of working age and older adults? *Clinical Psychology Review, 52,* 124–136.

Lewinsohn, P.M. (1974). A behavioural approach to depression. In R.M. Friedman & M.M. Katz (Eds.), *The psychology of depression: Contemporary theory and research* (pp. 157–185). Wiley.

Martell, C.R, Dimidjan, S. & Herman-Dunn, R. (2010). *Behavioural activation for depression: A clinician's guide.* Guilford Press.

Martell, C.R., Safren, S.A. & Prince, S.E. (2004.) *Cognitive-behavioural therapies with lesbian, gay and bisexual clients.* Guilford Press.

McKay, D., Sookman, D., Neziroglu, F., Wilhelm, S., Stein, D., Kyrio, M., Matthews, K. & Veale, D. (2015). Efficacy of cognitive-behavioral therapy for obsessive-compulsive disorder. *Psychiatry Research, 225*(3), 236–246.

Meichenbaum, D. (1969). The effect of instruction and reinforcement on thinking and language behaviours of schizophrenics. *Behaviour Research and Therapy, 7*(1), 101–114.

Meichenbaum, D. (1985). *Stress inoculation training.* Pergamon Press.

Moorey, S. & Lavender, A. (Eds.). (2019). *The therapeutic relationship in cognitive behavioural therapy.* Sage Publications.

National Institute for Health and Care Excellence (NICE). (2009). *Depression in adults: Recognition and management.* CG90. NICE.

Neenan, M. & Dryden, W. (2004). *Cognitive therapy: 100 key points.* Brunner-Routledge.

Newman, M.G., Castonguay, L.G., Borkovec, T.D., Fisher, A.J., Boswell, J.F., Szkodnyt, L.E. & Nordberg, S.S. (2011). A randomised controlled trial of cognitive behavioural therapy for generalised anxiety disorder with integrated techniques from emotion-focused and interpersonal therapies. *Journal of Consulting and Clinical Psychology, 79*(2), 171–181.

NHS England. (2019). *IAPT at 10: Achievements and challenges.* NHS England.

Olatunji, B.O., Cisler, J.M. & Deacon, B.J. (2010). Efficacy of cognitive behavioural therapy for anxiety disorders: A review of meta-analytic findings. *Psychiatry Clinics of North America, 33*(3), 557–577.

Ost, G. (1997). Rapid treatment of specific phobias. In G.C.L. Devey (Ed.), *Phobia: A handbook of theory, research and treatment* (pp. 227–246). Wiley.

Otto, M.W. & Deveney, C. (2005). Cognitive-behavioural therapy and the treatment of panic disorder: Efficacy and strategies. *The Journal of Clinical Psychiatry, 66*(4), 28–32.

Padesky, C.A. (1993). Schema as self-prejudice. *International Cognitive Therapy Newsletter, 5/6,* 16–17.

Padesky, C.A. & Beck, A.T. (2003). Science and philosophy: Comparison of cognitive therapy and rational emotive behaviour therapy. *Journal of Cognitive Psychotherapy, 17*(3), 211–224.

Padesky, C.A. & Beck, A.T. (2005). Response to Ellis' Discussion of 'Science and philosophy: Comparison of cognitive therapy and rational emotive behaviour therapy'. *Journal of Cognitive Psychotherapy, 19*(2), 187–192.

Padesky, C.A. & Greenberger, D. (2020). *Clinicians guide to using Mind Over Mood.* Guilford Press.

Padesky, C.A. & Mooney, K.A. (1990). Presenting the cognitive model to clients. *International Cognitive Therapy Newsletter, 6,* 13–14.

Pavlov, I.P. (1927). *Conditioned reflexes.* Oxford University Press.

Persons, J.B. (1989). *Cognitive therapy in practice: A case formulation approach.* W. W. Norton & Co.

Peteet, J.R. (2018). A fourth wave of psychotherapies: Moving beyond recovery towards well-being. *Harvard Review of Psychiatry, 26*(2), 90–95.

Prasko J., Divecky T., Grambal A., Kamaradova D., Mozny P., Sigmundova Z., Slepecky M. & Vyskocilova J. (2010). Transference and countertransference in cognitive behavioral therapy. *Biomedical papers of the Medical Faculty of the University Palacky, Olomouc, Czechoslovakia, 154*(3), 189–197.

Rachman, S. (2015). The evolution of behaviour therapy and cognitive behaviour therapy. *Behaviour Research and Therapy, 64*, 1–8.

Rachman, S.J. & Wilson, G.T. (1980). *The effects of psychological therapy* (2nd ed.). Pergamon.

Rauch, S.A.M., Eftekhari, A. & Ruzek, J.I. (2010). A review of exposure therapy: A gold standard for PTSD treatment. *Journal of Rehabilitation, Research & Development, 49*(5), 679–699.

Resick, P.A., Monson, C.M. & Chard, K.M. (2017). *Cognitive processing therapy for PTSD: A comprehensive manual.* Guilford Press.

Riddle-Walker, L., Veale, D., Chapman, C., Ogle, F., Rosko, D., Najmi, S., Walker, M., Maceachem, P. & Hicks, T. (2016). Cognitive behaviour therapy for specific phobia of vomiting (emetophobia): A pilot randomized controlled trial. *Journal of anxiety disorders, 43*, 14–22.

Rogers, C.R. (1957). The necessary and sufficient conditions of therapeutic personality change. *Journal of Consulting Psychology, 21*, 91–103. Reprinted in H. Kirschenbaum & V. L. Henderson (2000). *The Carl Rogers reader* (pp. 219–235). Constable.

Safran, J.D. & Segal, Z.V. (1990). *Interpersonal process in cognitive therapy.* Basic Books.

Salkovskis, P.M. (1985). Obsessional-compulsive problems: A cognitive-behavioural analysis. *Behaviour Research and Therapy, 23*, 571–583.

Simos, G. & Hofmann, S. (2013). *Cognitive therapy for anxiety disorders.* John Wiley & Sons.

Skinner, B.H. & Ferster, C.B. (1970). *Schedules of reinforcement.* Prentice-Hall, Inc.

Skinta, M. & Curtin, A. (2016). *Mindfulness and acceptance for gender and sexual minorities: A clinicians guide to fostering compassion, connection and equality, using contextual strategies.* New Harbinger.

Stone, L., Beck, A. & Hashempour, F. (2018). Introduction to the special issue on cultural adaptations of CBT. *The Cognitive Behaviour Therapist, 11*(15), 1–3.

Tarrier, N. & Johnson, J. (Eds.). (2016). *Case formulation in cognitive behaviour therapy: Treatment of challenging and complex cases* (2nd ed.). Routledge.

Thorndike, E.L. (1898). *Animal intelligence: An experimental study of the associative processes in animals.* American Psychological Association.

Thwaite, R. (Ed.). (2019). Special issue on cultural adaptation of CBT. *The Cognitive Behaviour Therapist 12*(40).

Tindall, L., Mikocka-Walus, A., Wright, B., Hewitt, C., Gascoyne, S. (2017). Is behavioural activation effective in the treatment of depression in young people? A systematic review and meta-analysis. *Psychological Psychotherapy: Theory, research and practice, 90*(4), 770–796.

Veale, D. & Neziroglu, F. (2010). *Body dysmorphia: A treatment manual.* John Wiley & Sons.

Veale, D. & Willson, R. (2005). *Overcoming obsessive compulsive disorder: A self-help guide using cognitive behavioural techniques.* Constable & Robinson.

Watson, J.B. & Rayner, R. (1920). Conditioned emotional reactions. *Journal of Experimental Psychology 3*, 1–14.

Williams, M. & Viscusi, J.A. (2016). Hoarding disorder and a systematic review of treatment with cognitive behavioral therapy. *Cognitive Behaviour Therapy, 45*(2), 93–110.

Wills, F. & Sanders, D. (1997). *Cognitive therapy: Transforming the image.* Sage.

Wolpe, J. (1958). *Psychotherapy by reciprocal inhibition.* Stanford University Press.

World Health Organization (WHO). (1990). *International classification of diseases* (10th rev.) (ICD-10). World Health Organization.

Young, J.E., Klosko, J.S. & Weishaar, M.E. (2003). *Schema therapy: A practitioner's guide.* Guilford Press.

Index

12-step approach 116

A
ABC
　forms 55
　in formulation 47
　model 18-20
　in REBT 12-13
acceptance (self/other) 18
　therapist, of client 38
acceptance and commitment
　　therapy (ACT) 114, 115
acting 'as if' 60-61
activating events 49 (*see also*
　　triggers)
active-directive, CBT as 22-23,
　　37, 100
addiction 16, 93
affect laden 31, 86,
agenda based, CBT as 22
agoraphobia 66, 113, 119, 138
ahistorical, CBT as 24
alliance concepts 36
American Psychiatric Association
　　(APA) 50, 68, 120
anorexia 114
anxiety/anxiety disorders 20-21,
　CBT for, 113, 119-120, 122
　and downward arrow
　　technique 87-88
　generalised, 113, 119, 122
　and goal setting 70-72
　health, 113
　IAPT and, 112-113
　and negative mental images 61
　and panic 50
　performance, 49
　postnatal, 114
　responses 10
　and safety behaviours 66-67
　social, 50, 71, 119, 123
　　case study 100ff
　and tasks 73-74
　'vicious flower' model of, 45-46
Association for Contextual and
　　Behavioural Science 115
assumptions 32
　adaptive, 95
　assessing, 79-81
　and behaviour change 95-96
　downward arrow and, 86-88
　dysfunctional 79, 83, 86
　maladaptive, 82-83, 95, 96
　rules and, 82
attentional bias 29
Aurelius 11
aversive emotions 65, 69
avoidance strategies 46, 66
　and behavioural activation 75
'awfulness', evaluation of 18, 19

B
Bandura, A. 10-11
Barlow, D.H. 119, 121, 122

Beck, A.T. 8, 11, 13, 14, 24, 36, 50, 65, 70, 76, 77, 121
Beck, J. 48
Beck Depression Inventory (BDI) 70
behaviour(s)
  maladaptive, 9, 38, 65
  mood-based, 68–69
behaviour(al)
  activation (BA) 66, 75–77, 115, 121, 122
  change 74, 75
  consequence 18, 19
  modification 10, 65, 72
  response(s) 28, 34, 35
  techniques 65ff, 98
  therapy 122
    influences on CBT 10
behaviourism 7
beliefs
  in ABC model 20, 55
  core, 31–35, 37, 40, 49, 58, 78, 86ff
    exposing 86
    formation of, 38, 48, 90
    maladaptive, 38, 56, 90
    reviewing change in, 95–96
  dysfunctional, 38
  functional, 63
  healthy, 27
  irrational, 12–13, 18
  maladaptive, 47, 95
  negative, 56–57, 65
  rational, 12–13, 18
  and triggers 96–97
Block, L. 11
body dysmorphic disorder 113, 120
Branch, R. 21, 40, 47, 60, 73
British Association for Behavioural and Cognitive Psychotherapies (BABCP) 113, 117
British Association for Counselling and Psychotherapy (BACP) 117
bulimia 114
Burdett, J. 5
Burns, D.D. 27

C

Canestrari, C. 40
case conceptualisation 44ff,
CBT
  as active-directive therapy 1, 22–23
  behaviour therapy influences on, 8–9
  characteristics of, 21–22
  with children and young people 114
  and client dependency 99
  cognitive therapy influences on, 8, 11–14
  collaborative emphasis 39, 40, 86, 93, 98
  computerised/online, 116–117
  and core conditions 36
  efficacy of, 119
    for anxiety disorders 119–120
    with black, Asian and minority ethnic populations 123
    for depression 121–122
    with LGBTQi+ 122–123
    for OCD 120–121
    with older adults 122
    for PTSD 121
  first session of, 70, 100
  fourth-wave, 115
  history of, 7–8

philosophical underpinnings
of, 11
research into, 118ff
second-wave, 114
self-help books 116
third-wave, 114
as two-person therapy 51
childhood experiences, significant
24, 32, 49
chronic
conditions 115, 122
efficacy of CBT for, 122
long-term CBT for, 21–22
and relapse 93
fatigue syndrome 114
pain 114, 115, 122
Cicero 11
Clark, D.M. 11, 50
client history 24
cognition 27ff, 52, 60, 65, 75, 86, 91
adaptive, 27
cognitive
aspects of depression 11
consequences 12, 18, 19, 21
dissonance 60, 61
distortions 28–30
model of emotional disorders 50
reconceptualisation 10–11
restructuring techniques 52ff, 60, 72, 76, 95, 119
therapy (CT) 8, 13
humour in, 40
influences on CBT 11–12
variables 10–11
collaboration 38, 39, 86
collaborative empiricism 39
compassion-focused therapy (CFT) 115
compensatory strategies 49, 65

conceptualisation(s)
basic, 44–46
case, 44ff, 50
detailed, 47–48
considerations when forming, 50–51
structured process of, 22, 50, 100
conditioned
response 9–10
stimulus 9–10
conditioning
classical, 8, 9
operant, 9, 10
congruence 36, 38
core
conditions 36, 37–39, 42
necessary and sufficient 36
schemata (*see* beliefs, core)
counselling 1ff,
and change 3
definition 2–3
and personal growth 6
Rogerian, 36–40
skills 100
countertransference 36, 42 (*see also* transference)
Covid-19 117
Covin, R. 119
Cox, D. 122
Craske, M.G. 119
Curtin, A. 123

D

daily thought records (DTRs) 53–55, 81
Davies, E. 5
demands, unreasonable 71
depression 3
behavioural activation and, 66, 75, 76, 77, 115

CBT as effective treatment for, 113, 118, 120–122
  in older adults 122
  with LGBTQI+ populations 123
 cognitive model of, 50
 cognitive therapy for, 11, 14, 76, 77
 as emotional consequence 18, 35
 IAPT approach to, 112–113
 mindfulness-based cognitive therapy for, 114
 severe, 65
 treatment-resistant, 93
desensitisation 10
Deveney, C. 119
dialectical behaviour therapy (DBT) 115
didactic teaching 22
Dionigi, A. 40
disputation 12, 25, 35
downward arrow, the 86–88, 90
Dobson, K.S. 11
D'Oyley, H. 122
Dryden, W. 21, 40, 47, 60, 73, 78
DSM-IV-TR 68, 120
DSM-5 50, 68, 120

E

eating disorders 114
Ellis, A. 7–8, 11, 12, 13, 18, 21, 40
emotional
 change 61, 74
 consequence 16, 17–19, 55, 82–83
  depression as, 18
 disturbance 16–17, 21, 30, 50, 53
 and intrusive images 62
 problems and core beliefs 33–34
 reasoning 29
 response(s) 10, 11, 12, 20, 28, 34–35, 47, 56, 82
  therapist's to client 42
emotions
 aversive, 65, 69
 functional, 20–21
 negative dysfunctional, 16–17, 18, 20–21, 60, 96, 97
 within an interactive system 65, 71–72, 94
empathy 36, 37
endings 92ff, 98–99
environmental factors 21, 24, 44, 49, 73, 94, 96
Epictetus 11, 17
experimental approach (in CBT) 23

F

feelings 16ff
 interaction with thoughts and behaviours 12, 53
 strategies to avoid, 69–70
Ferster, C.B. 75
Foa, E.B. 121
Franklin, M.E. 120, 121
Friborg, O. 122

G

Gilbert, P. 42–43, 115
goal(s)
 oriented (CBT) 24
 reviewing, 24, 94–95, 98
 setting, 22, 24, 70–75
 SMART, 70–71
GPs 98
Greenberger, D. 31
Guasp, A. 123
guided discovery 24

The Primers in Counselling Series by PCCS Books

This best-selling series offers comprehensive descriptions of key counselling approaches and contexts in the 21st century. Accessible and concise, they are ideal for students seeking a theory bridge between introductory, intermediate and diploma courses or for comparative essays and integrative theory assignments.

The other primers in the series are:

The Focusing-Oriented Counselling Primer (2nd edition) – Campbell Purton   pbk 9781915220004 – epub 9781915220011

The Rational Emotive Behaviour Therapy Primer – Windy Dryden   pbk 9781910919965 – epub 9781910919972

The Pluralistic Therapy Primer – Kate Smith and Ani de la Prida   pbk 9781910919866 – epub 9781910919873

The Single-Session Counselling Primer – Windy Dryden   pbk 9781910919569 – epub 9781910919583

The Existential Counselling Primer (2nd edition) – Mick Cooper   pbk 9781910919750 – epub 9781910919767

The Person-Centred Counselling Primer – Pete Sanders   pbk 9781898059806 – epub 9781906254841

The Integrative Counselling Primer – Richard Worsley   pbk 9781898059813 – epub 9781906254902

The Experiential Counselling Primer – Nick Baker   pbk 9781898059837

The Contact Work Primer: Introduction to pre-therapy – edited by Pete Sanders: pbk 9781898059844

The Psychodynamic Counselling Primer – Mavis Klein   pbk 9781898059851 – epub 9781906254896

Discounted prices and free UK P&P – www.pccs-books.co.uk